all the men
I've ever dated.
Especially
the last one.

CELIBACY
Is Better Than
Really Bad
SEX

And Other Classic Rules
For Single Women

by Patti Putnicki

CorkScrew Press ❖ Los Angeles
Distributed by The Globe Pequot Press

CORKSCREW PRESS®

Published by CorkScrew Press, Inc.
4470-107 Sunset Blvd., Suite 234
Los Angeles, California 90027

Distributed by The Globe Pequot Press
P.O. Box 833
Old Saybrook, CT 06475-0833

Distributed in Canada by General Publishing, Don Mills, Ontario.

Cover design by Ken Niles, *Ad Infinitum*, Santa Monica, California.

Library of Congress Cataloging-in-Publication Data

Putnicki, Patti.
    Celibacy is better than really bad sex : and other rules for single women / by Patti Putnicki.
      p. cm.
    ISBN 0-944042-35-X (pbk.)
    1. Single women—Humor. 2. Sexual abstinence— Humor. 3. Sex—Humor. I. Title.
    PN6231.S5485P98 1994 818'.5402—dc20 94-33737

For single-copy orders, see page 169, or call 1-800-243-0495.
For quantity discounts, please write to the distributor.

Trademarks used in this book are property of various trademark owners.

Resemblance of any character in this book to any person — living or dead — is purely coincidental, but if you recognize anyone you know in here, buy this book and give it to him.

Printed in the U.S.A.

10   9   8   7   6   5   4   3   2   1

C O N T E N T S

CELIBACY
Is Better Than
Really Bad
SEX

Introduction

URING MY 20's, I CREATED THE PERFECT MENTAL portrait of my future husband. He'd have a Mel Gibson mug, a Jay Leno wit, and the brain power of a five-time Jeopardy champion. He'd exude social charm, epitomize business savvy, and dress like a GQ supermodel. Most importantly, he'd be romantic — complete with candlelight dinners, charged words of devotion, and an honorary membership in FTD's Frequent Floral Program.

By the time I turned 30, I had dated every man south of the Mason-Dixon line who met these requirements (there were seven).

"Sorry, no date, but have some Godiva, lady."

In the process, I'd amassed a closetful of pastel-from-hell bridesmaid gowns with propeller-sized butt-bows, attended more baby showers than Barney, and discovered that my only hope for a candlelight dinner was a Bigfoot pizza at the home of a man who'd missed one too many electric bills. If I paid for the pizza.

That's when I became a little more realistic. As I reshuffled my priorities and reevaluated my standards, I realized that my true marital dream mate really needed just two character traits to set my heart aflame: 1) a great sense of humor, and, 2) the energy to brush after every meal — even those eaten over the sink.

My friends, now married, think I've set my sights too high. And this mysterious knight of oral hygiene eludes me still.

SINGLE AFTER 30. I'M BLAMING MY THIGHS.

Here's the Catch-22 of being single — especially after 30. As soon as you learn to recognize Mr. Right, he immediately becomes harder to find. The stakes get higher, your chest sags lower, and, to top it all off, you must continue your soulmate odyssey ser-enaded by a ringing chorus of, "You're such a [*pretty/funny/smart/sensitive/rich/talented*] woman, why aren't you married?" As if you purposely emit some estrogen vapor that keeps the nice guys away.

What's more, married people feel a social obligation to give you their heartfelt advice on the subject, and will continue to do so until you go to your grave — or register at Bloomingdale's — whichever comes first.

To say I've been there would be an understatement. I live there. You live there. In a world of "promising" dates who'll soon

Who will he be?
What will he
look like?

pass up a Victoria's Secret surprise for the next inning of mid-season baseball. In a universe of blind dates who look like they stepped right out of a Vincent Price movie. And in a country where guys go high-tailing back to 50-pound overweight controlling ex-wives, even though you've lived on a steady diet of Slimfast and tolerance for 363 fat-free days. It just leaves you wondering if there's really someone for everyone — and fearful that *your* someone is currently living half-a-world away, pondering a sex-change operation.

YOU'RE SINGLE. BUT YOU'RE NOT ALONE.

It's enough to scare the living daylights out of Stephen King. The bizarre dates. The psycho matchmakers. And the friends who now refer to your marital status as your "situation," as if it were some global disaster on the evening news. We become reluctant poster children, surrounded by well-meaning mantras of "don't worry, you'll meet someone" — just when you start feeling pretty good about being single. Trust me, you *will* meet someone. There's just no telling who —

or *what*. But until then, the unsolicited advice will continue to pump faster than hairspray at a singles bar.

Perhaps you, too, have been the lucky recipient of that choice Oprah transcript, mailed anonymously by some well-meaning friend. The show about women who are too ambitious, too vulnerable, too independent — or women whose whole lives were changed by a dental procedure, a vegetarian cooking class, a sex guru, or a visit from alien creatures they eventually chose to marry.

Or the phone call from Mom bearing news of a "charming new single guy next door" — a parolee released for good behavior — "who's really nice to his mother and just needs a good woman to get his life back on track."

After one night at a singles bar, church social or "people without partners" pity party, maybe you wish you had taken down his number.

But don't dial 1-900-Howard-Stern for advice. Being single can be more than tolerable. In fact, it can be fun. It all depends on your attitude. The first thing you have to remember is you're not alone.

Just think
of this as continuing
education. A compilation
of the universal rules of
dating that will help you keep
your sense of humor, self-esteem
and personal sanity as you
continue to pass through
"Go" in the dating
game of life.

Second, you never will be. After all, you've got people inviting you to parties just to hear your bizarre dating tales. A few more bad relationships, and you can start charging a cover.

Granted, the whole thing would be a lot easier if someone had told us the rules would change. If they'd just shown us the "Dating After 30" documentary in conjunction with the "Birds & Bees" filmstrip in fifth grade health class.

But they didn't. Which is why you're reading this book. Just think of it as continuing education. A compilation of the universal rules of dating that will help you keep your sense of humor, self-esteem and personal sanity as you continue to pass through "Go" in the dating game of life.

Rules like, "If you leave no stone unturned, you're bound to find a guy who's been living under a rock."

Now, isn't this more fun than group therapy?

Sticks & Stones Can Break Your Bones

(but annoying married statements can amuse you)

EVENTUALLY, SOMEONE, SOMEWHERE, WILL THOUGHTLESSLY HURL A DAMN (Dumb Annoying Married Notion) in your general direction. If not handled correctly, one DAMN statement can propel you within inches of a suite at the Betty Ford Clinic — or a cell on death row — depending on your current mental state or the availability of lethal weapons. Your best bet is to take a deep breath, ponder the DAMN statement, recognize its stupidity, and thank your lucky stars you'll never be married to the person who made it.

GUESS WHO'S *STILL* NOT MARRIED?!

How to ward off the worst of the DAMN statements

Use these defensive measures to deflect any Dumb Annoying Married Notions thrown at you.

OFFENSE	YOUR BEST DEFENSE
"You're not getting any younger, dear."	Remind them that the aging process is not exclusive to singles. In fact, studies prove it often occurs more rapidly in married people.
"If you don't hurry up, all the single men will be gone."	Suggest the two of you drive by the county courthouse during divorce decree day and gawk at the recyclables. If you see something you like, offer ten cents a pound.
"I don't understand why you're still not married."	Chances are, this individual also doesn't understand solar energy, the budget deficit, or why you spent $48 on thigh cream, either.

OFFENSE	YOUR BEST DEFENSE
"Why don't you go out with [*Name of Potential Hell Date here*]. **What's the worst that can happen?"**	Explain that's exactly how Ms. Hun met Attilla, Ms. Limbaugh met Rush, and Ms. Rodham met Bill. (This is especially effective if this is how the DAMN person met the current spouse.).
"How can you stay single when *EVERYONE'S* getting married?"**	Remember, *EVERYONE* bought bellbottoms, Epiladys and Dalkon shields at some point, too.
"Everyone should have children."**	Proudly exhibit your personal laminated letter from Sally Struthers thanking you for your generous donation, and the 8 x 10 glossy of Duc Tape, your foster daughter from Phumi Blanc, Cambodia. Then smile.
"Maybe you're just too picky."**	Bring the first loser you meet to this person's next party. Watch the reactions as he parks his rusty Pinto on the front lawn, heads straight for the booze, and starts hitting on your friend's wife.
"I hope you're lucky enough to meet someone as wonderful as [*Spouse's Name Here*]."**	Thank this person for making you realize just how truly lucky you are to be single.

The Biggest Lie You'll Ever Tell Is *"Never Again"*

I T'S TRUE. SINGLE WOMEN LIE. "I *LOVE* FOOTBALL." "W*HAT* BALD spot??" "I *wasn't* faking." Those little things that keep a relationship going until you realize it's going nowhere. But the biggest lie we ever tell is the one we tell ourselves. You know it. You've said it many times. It's *"Never Again."*

"Never Again." It's the cream center on the Oreo of failed relationships. The Band-Aid for the blind date who arrived with his mother in the back seat because she owns the car. The salve on the burn of "this could be the one" who never called again.

"Never Again." That's single-female-speak for "maybe next time." Because there always will be a next time. Followed by another *"Never Again."*

I think the technical term for it is "dating."

I wonder if he's geographically desirable?

NEVER AGAIN

The 12 Steps of *Never Again.**

1. Have bad relationship or psycho date from hell.
2. Scream *"Never Again"* while eating something high in fat.
3. Stop shaving your legs.
4. Watch *Thelma & Louise* 25 times.
5. Focus on friends, career, volunteer work and novel.
6. State loudly and clearly to any person who happens to cross your path that you're perfectly happy being single.
7. Watch *The Way We Were, Casablanca* or *Three's Company* and get sentimental.
8. Start fantasizing about Barney Rubble.
9. Spy a cute guy.
10. Start shaving your legs.
11. Get a complete makeover, buy a new outfit and enroll in aerobics.
12. Go back to the place you saw the cute guy, smile, and entice him to ask you out.

*Repeat steps one through twelve throughout your single life.

The
Single Female's
Dating
Rating Quiz

Honestly, which of the choices was:

More fun?

☐ Your last date

☐ Shopping for a bathing suit

More entertaining?

☐ Your last date

☐ Your last mammogram

More exciting?

☐ Your last date

☐ Al Gore

More romantic?

☐ Your last date

☐ An FTD ad

More long-term potential?

☐ Your last date

☐ Your last manicure

Most likely to send you a card by mail?

☐ Your last date

☐ Your insurance agent

Most likely to show up in your fantasies?

☐ Your last date

☐ Mel Gibson

☐ Mrs. Fields

> ## BONUS QUESTION

After going out with this guy more than once, did you swear this was:

☐ Your last date

The Road To Happy Hour Is Paved With Spandex

IF YOU REALLY THINK ABOUT WHAT YOU HAVE TO GO THROUGH TO meet eligible guys, even the most liberated woman can start to long for the days of arranged marriages. Particularly if you've ever been to Happy Hour.

First, your romantic fantasy meeting probably doesn't include seeing Mr. Right's butt planted on a barstool. Second, if your asset is your personality, it's hard to compete with women who look like you did at 18 — only cuter and dumber.

So, if you venture into the swizzle stick sector, you've got to be ready to compete — by donning the dreaded mating fabric guaranteed to release the "Hey Baby" endorphin in Mr. Right.

That fabric is Spandex.

Although easy-to-pack in an eyeglass case and virtually wrinkle-free, Spandex comes with its share of problems. You've got to pour your entire body into a garment that's no bigger than a can of Slimfast. And you've got to do it before Last Call.

Successful Spandex dressing strategies

1. Eat and drink nothing for two days.
2. Try to stop breathing at least three hours before Happy Hour begins.
3. Have all moles, freckles and insect bites surgically removed.
4. Make sure you're not anywhere close to having to use the bathroom.
5. Lie on your bed and scoontch your body into trendy Spandex outfit.
6. Straighten any seams that are now spiraling around your thigh.
7. Hop in place until crotch moves from kneecap region to target area.
8. Accessorize with seductive earrings.
9. Continue holding breath.
10. Drive to Happy Hour standing up.

> ## The most common uses of Spandex
>
> 1. Holding things in.
> 2. Pushing things out.
> 3. Performing *Swan Lake.*

If you've been out of the proverbial bar scene for some time, you may find it difficult to feel sexy when you're dressed like Captain Kirk. However, the more significant problem occurs if you have anything less than a jumbo-sized bladder.

SPANDEX DISASSEMBLY STRATEGIES

At some point during the evening, you'll find yourself bolting from your barstool to the Ladies Room, only to realize that disassembling your outfit requires the skill of a federal bomb squad, and about the same number of people. You'll also discover that Spandex fibers are magically drawn to water, and that a big portion of your ensemble will somehow end up soaking in the toilet without your knowledge.

Unless you spend a good half-hour crouched under the hot air dryer, you'll return from the Ladies Room looking as if you've just gone diving with Jacques Cousteau. Further, the hot air dryer will have caused major shrinkage, which now means your trendy Spandex outfit can be donated to a halfway house for wayward

Garment designed to release the "Hey Baby" endorphin in Victorian Mr. Right.

Keebler elves. Not that anyone will notice, though. You've spent so much time in the bathroom that the bar is now closed.

This is why every Spandex outfit should come with a free catheter.

MAKEUP GUIDELINES FOR HAPPY HOUR HOPEFULS

Applying appropriate Happy Hour makeup is relatively simple. Just observe some of the choice examples around you: *apply makeup until you look like you've been run over by a Maybelline truck. Continue applying in the Ladies Room just in case the wind took a gallon or two of liner off your lids.*

It also helps to roll around in five or six bottles of your favorite perfume. This doesn't attract men, but it does drown out the smell of their five or six bottles of aftershave.

LAST-MINUTE HAPPY HOUR MAKEUP CHECKLIST

1. Do I look like Madonna — or at least a Mary Kay sales rep?
2. Is lipstick circling my face? Is it a frosted color?
3. Can people living in Beijing smell my fragrance?
4. Are my eyelashes long enough to impale the bartender?

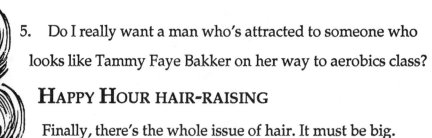

5. Do I really want a man who's attracted to someone who looks like Tammy Faye Bakker on her way to aerobics class?

HAPPY HOUR HAIR-RAISING

Finally, there's the whole issue of hair. It must be big. At least big enough to qualify as a multiple-family dwelling. If you live anywhere in the South, it should qualify as an apartment. And it should be sprayed till it's at least as sturdy as Mount Rushmore.

You should also carry additional hairspray with you to Happy Hour to:

1. Perform touch-ups.
2. Blind any woman who may be considered competition.

NOW YOU'RE READY FOR HAPPY HOUR!

You're filled with hope. Stuffed into Spandex. Camouflaged by concealer. And topped by a pile of hair that could qualify as a national monument.

And you wonder if, maybe, possibly, *this* time, you'll actually meet a guy who'll like you for the real you.

"Can I borrow your hairspray?"

If He Says His Wife Doesn't Understand Him, Suggest He Enroll In Berlitz

YOU'RE DESTINED TO MEET THREE TYPES OF MARRIED MEN AT Happy Hour:

1. Men who tell you they're married.

2. Men who pretend they're not married.

3. Men who don't know for sure.

All these men work in different professions and wear diverse wardrobes. They all engage in fascinating hobbies and profess varying political opinions. But they all have one thing in common. They are married to the same woman. You know the one.

That "wife who doesn't understand me."

...and then she has the nerve to tell me to take out the trash *AND* walk the dog — in the rain. And after a hard day at work! She has no idea what I have to put up with at the office. And what does *SHE* do all day? *Huh?* And then, to top it all off, she's too tired at night to take care of, um, y'know, ME. We haven't had sex in *five* months, not that I'm all that attracted to her anymore. You wouldn't believe how she's rea[?] let herself go — an[?] won't do a damn th[?] about it. If If I'd ha[?] known what she [?] going to loo[?] like when I [?] married her [?] I probably would have had a lot o[?] second thoughts a[?]

This woman *really* gets around!

She nags constantly. Spends too much of his hard-earned money. And she's completely occupied with the kids. She's stopped cooking dinner. Grown torpedo-sized saddlebags. And keeps the house like a pigsty. What's more, she has no interest in sex. None whatsoever. Zippo. *Nada.* Not even on his birthday.

I think it's completely understandable. This woman must be *exhausted.* Marching down aisle after aisle without a break, hurling bouquets like Olympic shotputs, writing thank-you cards with the speed of a laser printer — all the while consuming enough wedding cake to throw anyone else into an irreversible sugar coma. People get their pictures on postage stamps for less.

If I had my way, I'd take up a collection for this woman and give her a well-deserved vacation. In my book, she's earned it.

I'd also make it illegal for men to discuss "The Wife Who Doesn't Understand Me" under the guise of "Happy Hour." After all,

Unhappy Hour

you don't have to be married to be misunderstood.

The phone company doesn't understand ME when I dispute a $7,874.22 long-distance charge for a six-hour phone call to Fiji I'm pretty sure I would have remembered. The garage mechanic doesn't understand me when I tell him the engine makes a noise like an earring-back falling on a hardwood floor when I make a right-hand turn. And the cashier at the 7-Eleven doesn't understand me — *ever*.

I know you have your own list of people who don't understand you. Maybe that's why you went to Happy Hour in the first place. And that's why you're no longer obligated to respond to the man who says his wife doesn't understand *him*.

You just don't speak the same language.

In his world, the words "happy hour" translate into "I've told my wife I'm at a meeting." In yours, it means "sixty minutes with a married bore who's going through mid-life crisis while I'm downing alcoholic beverages and wishing I'd really stayed home to watch reruns of Murphy Brown and enjoy the company of Ben & Jerry."

Cheers!

There Will Always Be A Larry Newman

O MATTER WHAT PART OF THE COUNTRY YOU VISIT, NO matter how chic the bar might be, you will always meet a Larry Newman.

He's the guy who holds entire conversations with your chest, claims he invented the Today Sponge, and insists you and he were lovers in a past life. All things Larry Newman actually believes.

Though seemingly harmless and sometimes mildly amusing in a Stephen King sort of way, Larry Newman can throw a major kink into your single life. This is because Larry Newman thinks the two of you are actually hitting it off. Larry Newman believes that you've excused yourself to go to the phone and call your

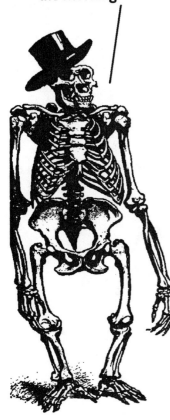

...are you an omelette kind of girl, or would you like pancakes in the morning?

Early New-Magnon Man

mother to tell her you've finally met the man you're going to marry. And Larry Newman believes he's going to get lucky tonight. *Verrrry* lucky.

In fact, Larry Newman will stop at nothing to relay these facts to the entire bar while you're innocently struggling to rearrange your Spandex unitard in the Ladies Room. Which means you'll return to a bar where the nice guys are questioning your judgement, and the other Larry Newmans are trying to figure out how to get your phone number. And you'll spend the rest of the evening wondering why.

You see, the sad thing is, normal methods of rejection won't keep away the Larry Newmans of the world. The glaring looks, the put-down lines — even the smell of garlic — only fuels the hormonal fires in the Happy Hour Don Juan of Delusion. Although women are gifted with the power of procreation and the perils of PMS, we're genetic mutants when it comes to having innate Larry Newman repellent.

The only answer to the problem is run — run like the wind — to another bar crawling with the type of losers and low-lifes you're better equipped to handle.

The Lines You'll Hear At Happy Hour Will Never Be Deeper Than Those Around Your Eyes

Wush cookin' good lookin'?

ONCE YOU'VE EXPERIENCED THE UNHAPPILY MARRIEDS, THE LARRY Newmans and the World's Oldest Conventioneer — who swears you look just like The Bubble Lady from the old Lawrence Welk Show — you've earned the opportunity to meet and mingle with other delightful singles in the bar. You'll quickly find yourself drawn into earnest conversations on social injustice. Healthcare reform. Nuclear disarmament. And Wall Street scandals. Heated debates on the World Series, gays in the military, gun control and the standardization of European economies. All of which will begin when a mysterious stranger walks over to pose one all-important question to you.

"What's your sign?"

Because you're a woman who values her time, it's important for you to remember one vital fact. A man *can* be judged by his pick-up line. It's actually a better indicator of his position in life and his true mental abilities than the color of his credit card.

The Clip 'n' Carry Pick-up Line Decoder

Use these defensive measures to deflect any unwanted opening lines aimed your way.

PICK-UP LINE	WHAT IT REALLY MEANS
"What's your sign?"	This man is recently divorced and has not dated since The Age of Aquarius. Continue this conversation only if your name is Astral Daylilly.
"Can I borrow a cigarette?"	This man will talk to you for three-and-one-half hours, yet never buy you a drink. This is probably because he is unemployed. *Do not let him see your Gold Card.*

PICK-UP LINE	WHAT IT REALLY MEANS
"You have really great biceps."	This man is a personal trainer. Proceed with caution unless your idea of a romantic dinner involves brown rice followed by a hot, sweaty ride on a Nautilus machine.
"W-e-e-e-l-l-l, what have we here?	This man is a space alien and has never seen a woman before. Smile only if you have the urge to visit Pluto.
"Do you know where a guy could get scrod in this town?"	This man just came from losing amateur night at The Improv. Don't wait for him to tell you another joke. He IS the joke.
"Ain't you a cute li'l thang."	This man's name is Tex. Continue this conversation only if you have an impetuous urge to ride in the back of a pick-up with a dog named Gus.
"Hello, my name is...."	*Congratulations!* You may have just met your future husband.

Never Bring A Married Friend To Happy Hour

Y OU MAY HAVE BEEN FRIENDS SINCE COLLEGE. YOU MAY HAVE shared your innermost secrets, your most intimate fears, your wildest dreams. You may even trust this person with your life.

This is fine. Just never take this married friend to Happy Hour. *Never*. Because she will make an attempt to help.

Even the most nailed-down married friend turns into your Great Aunt Sylvia at the mere sight of a swizzle stick. Before you order your first round, she'll embark on an endless mission to retrieve every single male within a six-mile radius, and drag each of them (sometimes with force) to perch on the barstool next to you.

As they make their visual inspection, she'll relay a rote monologue of your vital statistics, including your hobbies, interests, annual salary and family of origin — ending with the leading question, "Can you BELIEVE someone like her STILL isn't married?"

Barstools Should Come With Ejection Seats

SOME WOMEN BELIEVE THAT EVERY MAN WHO VENTURES INTO A singles bar is a jerk. Others believe that every man on this planet is a jerk. Neither statement is true.

In fact, nice guys *do* go to singles bars — typically on the very same night you're in aerobics class, working overtime or waxing your legs. These nice guys then leave, totally dejected, wondering why all the women they met that evening were dim-witted, money-hungry or bursting out of their Spandex. Later that evening, they'll be lamenting this situation with their buddies over pizza and beer at precisely the same moment you're leaving your driveway for the very same bar they just left.

It's a cruel twist of the Happy Hour drink garnish. Proof that

God has a sense of humor. And validation of the cliche that timing is everything.

After an hour or so of Messrs. "I-Can't-Believe-This-Guy's-For-Real," most intelligent single women will experience a passage. Five distinct stages now recognized by noted psychologists throughout the world. Stages that may one day be sanctioned by *Cosmo*. I call this passage "The Five Stages of Single Bar Blues."

The ⑤ Stages Of Singles Bar Blues

Stage One
Anticipation

The joyous, childlike hope that you will meet exciting, intelligent, delightful men who will recognize your sparkling personality and striking good looks.

Stage Two
Acceptance

The reality-driven resignation that you'd be happy to meet a member of the male species who refrains from calling you "babe."

Stage Three
Denial

The total inability to believe you're attracting every obnoxious, mentally unstable, multi-tatooed or mildewed man in the bar. You may mistakenly accuse the bartender of using a hidden camera to tape your evening in an attempt to win $10,000 on "America's Funniest Videos."

Stage Four
Retreat

The quick exit to the Ladies Room to ponder the prospect of a) losing ten pounds, b) changing perfumes, c) investing in implants/dental bonding/tummy tucks/thigh cream, d) moving out of state and/or e) entering the convent.

Stage Five
Defeat

The consumption of an entire two-pound bag of fudge-covered Oreos at home while pondering life-long solitaire and listening to the New Age version of "Feelings" you impulsively ordered from the Home Shopping Club.

Amazing Secret Remedy!

Proven by millions of women to be 95% effective in instantly countering the effects of the Single Bar Blues.

At Stage Two, you have two options. Either cry in your cocktail — or sit back and enjoy the show: count the Spandex panty lines. Add up the hair plugs. Guess the waitresses' natural hair color. Count how many times the word "party" is used as a verb. Analyze the ratio of male pattern baldness versus breast implants. Identify which animal each bar inhabitant most closely resembles (pay special attention to the ones eating peanuts). Secretly vote for "the most likely to succeed." Imagine the bar patrons as a mobile sculpture. At least now, you can write the evening off as a cultural experience.

Punch-Out & Carry

No-Pest Strips

for Happy Hour Emergencies

THESE DAYS, YOU'RE NO LONGER REQUIRED TO SPEND MORE THAN FIVE minutes with any man you've pegged as "unfit" or "unclean" while waiting to create an excuse to make a subtle exit.

Simply clip out these handy "No-Pest Strips" — carry them behind the Macy's card in your wallet — and flash 'em when the moment is right (and you're relatively certain Mr. Wrong can read).

Because these strips are the size of business cards, it's a rather humane way to get your message across, because other guys at the bar will think you're giving Mr. Wrong your phone number. In fact, if Mr. Wrong is drunk enough, he may even think the same thing.

IT'S AGAINST MY RELIGION TO DATE A HAIRLESS MAN.

CAUTION: IQ OVER 100.

YOU MUST HAVE ME CONFUSED WITH SOMEONE NAMED BAMBI.

 MORE...

...really bad SEX • 47

No-Pest Strips

SPECIAL BONUS SECTION!

I WOULD RATHER SLEEP WITH MY BROTHER.

I VOTED FOR CLINTON.

I BURIED MY LAST FOUR HUSBANDS.

PLEASE LEAVE. YOU'RE MAKING ME FRIGID.

MY REAL NAME IS LORENA BOBBITT.

NOTE: Extra cards can be sold in the Ladies Room for a huge profit — especially during convention season.

Sleepless in Seattle
Is A Sick Illusion
(unless you look like Meg Ryan)

MANY PEOPLE CRIED WHEN THEY SAW *SLEEPLESS IN SEATTLE*. ME? I scowled. You see, I had a lot of questions. Like, how did Tom Hanks afford that great house? Which employer — short of the government — lets an employee expense out a personal trip? Why wasn't it as realistic as *When Harry Met Sally*? And, more significantly, would Tom Hanks have been so enamored with the Meg Ryan character if she'd have been played by Roseanne? Or me?

I think not.

Okay, so I gave the movie two thumbs down. But it brought up an interesting point. If you can't meet Mr. Right at the usual places — like Happy Hour or on top of the Empire State Building — where the heck are you *supposed* to meet him?

TAKE THE ALTERNATE ROUTE TO SINGLE-MINGLING

Month after month, I see articles about the "Hot New Meeting Spots For Singles"— places ranging from the car wash and the grocery store to the health club and the DMV. This does not make meeting men any easier. It does, however, mean that I now have to dress in full regalia just to go buy a box of Grape Nuts.

Now, I can't leave the house to pick up the paper without my eyeliner in place — Mr. Right could be jogging by. "Who knows?" say the magazines. "He may just invite you to brunch." Once again, I think not.

I thought they were going to send the young one.

I have tried these alternative meeting places. In fact, I've spent so much time getting ready to run errands, that my dry cleaning's been given to charity and my coupons have expired before I reached the checkout counter. And the only proposition I've received is from the detail man at the car wash. Either that, or he was signaling me to claim my Honda.

Maybe *you* will have better luck today.

Alternative "Hot New Meeting Spots" for adventurous singles

An essential supplement to suggestions you'll find in many women's magazines.

Car Wash

Look for the following clues before you ask Mr. Hangin'-Around Waiting-For-His-Car for advice on your next lube: make of his car, visible signs of car seats, stuffed animals or fuzzy dice, and how many times he uses his cellular phone while waiting for his wax job.

Grocery Store

First assess his shopping cart for total fat content, prescription drugs, movie rentals and condom purchases. Stay away from those containing fried pork rinds, lithium, *Wrestlemania* and Trojanettes

---

Health Clubs

Beware of any man who's chest is larger than yours.

Dry Cleaner	Although it's easy to evaluate a man's marital status and taste in clothes by scrutinizing his order, I've never found a way to detain a man at a dry cleaners short of hooking him with a hanger or tripping him with a plastic bag.
Home Depot	Sure, there are lots of guys there, but no woman alive can compete with a Rigid Tool.
Bookstore	Great place to find guys who can read. Stay away from the ones buying, *The Twelve-Step Program For Men Who Hate Women With Jobs*, *Barney's Big Adventure* and *Recognizing The Sadistic You*.
Department Store TV Section	Don't bother. All these guys are married.
Laundromat	Do you really want a guy who can't afford a washer-dryer?

Why read an entire book when you can get the Cliffs Notes?

101 Things NOT To Say During Sex???

Lights! Camera!
Action??

If all you're getting at the car wash lately is dirty looks, you can always take a shot at video dating. The high-tech mating ground of the '90s. The virtual reality arranged marriage without the traditional exchange of burros. The pay-per-view, man-of-the-month club, complete with  home movies. It's *hip*. It's *now*. And it's got to be as embarrassing as your mother showing your baby pictures to your prom date. Except now, you don't have your mother to blame.

I like the concept of video dating as much as I liked the plot of *Sleepless in Seattle*. But, then again, I'm the one who gets dressed up to go to the recycling center just in case Mr. Right is environmentally conscientious. So who am I to judge? All I can say is if you enter the wacky world of video dating, at least be prepared.

Try this script for successful video dating.

HI! I'M (*your name here, first name only*). I'M KINDA NERVOUS BECAUSE I'VE NEVER DONE ANYTHING LIKE THIS BEFORE (*nervous giggle*). LET'S SEE, I'M (*height*) AND WEIGH ABOUT (*your actual weight minus 13 pounds*). I LOVE TO (*fill in a couple of hobbies*) AND TAKE LONG WALKS IN THE MOONLIGHT. IN MY SPARE TIME, I (*make something up that's environmentally correct, such as brewing tea from bark*). AND EVERY NIGHT, I PRAY FOR WORLD PEACE. I'M LOOKING FOR A MAN WHO'S BREATHING, SINGLE AND IS KIND TO ALL LIVING CREATURES, UNLESS IT'S DURING FOOTBALL SEASON. IF YOU FIT THE BILL, GIVE ME A CALL AND TELL ME ABOUT YOURSELF. AND IF YOU'RE ONE OF THE GUYS FROM THE LAUNDROMAT, YOU SHOULD SAVE THE MONEY YOU'RE SPEND-ING ON THIS DATING SERVICE AND BUY A WASHER-DRYER. YOU'RE 40 YEARS OLD, FOR GOD'S SAKE.

Hey, you may not find a guy, but if you send the tape to Ed McMahon, you might be the winning spokesmodel on *Starsearch...*

If You Meet The Man Of Your Dreams On An Airplane, A Flight Attendant Named Gretchen Will Immediately Seat An Unescorted Child Between You

PERHAPS YOU ARE NOT FAMILIAR WITH INTERNATIONAL AIRLINE law as it applies to single women.

First, you will always have a flight attendant trainee named Gretchen — a woman who shifts the focus of every man on the plane toward her because Gretchen looks just like Elle McPherson in her younger years. Only better. Gretchen will not give you a full can of Diet Coke. Gretchen will not find you a blanket. And Gretchen will not let you get past the beverage cart to go to the bathroom. Gretchen will, however, seat Erick — the unescorted demon child — in the middle seat beside you, and appoint you as his legal guardian the entire time you're on the plane.

Gretchen can do this.

It's international airline law.

Erick's mission in life is to ensure you remain single for the rest of your natural days. He comes perfectly equipped to perform this assignment, toting the official Bart Simpson annoyance kit, which contains at least 14 Ding Dongs, 11 Hostess Sno Balls with extra cream filling, and every electronic or injury-producing toy a thoughtless parent can purchase. All of which he'll unpack before the seatbelt demonstration, consume or break before the oxygen-mask video, and repair or spit up before take-off. Erick, who is naturally hyper, has now produced enough adrenaline to power the DC-10 you're on — unless he somehow goes into insulin shock during the raucous celebration of his 48th victory in Super Mario Brothers.

After only 15 minutes as Erick's seatmate and surrogate mother, you no longer have the urge to flirt with Prince Charming in the window seat. You're more concerned about getting the Ding Dong goo out of your spectator pumps. More focused on bandaging a three-inch gash over your eye (due to Erick's unprecedented demonstration of the pop-fly capabilities of an aluminum can when hit with a rolled up copy of *Business Week*). More centered on the hand-molded likeness of Ninja Turtles (created from today's leftover breakfast service) which is hurtling toward your lap, thanks to Erick's need to practice some juvenile version of the limbo with his table tray.

Your in-flight libido has now taken a nose-dive. It's been totally replaced by the urge to scrape hardened food remnants from your Anne Klein IIs.

THIS IS THE MOMENT YOUR OXYGEN MASK SHOULD DROP DOWN

Meanwhile, the other passengers think you're just another cruel parent ignoring her poor child. Prince Charming thinks you require psychiatric care. And Gretchen is lamenting her broken nail to the fifteen men hovering around the galley.

When the plane finally lands — with security officers meeting you at the gate for questioning — you're bound to notice Mr. Charming handing his business card to Gretchen, the flight atten-

dant trainee. You'll calmly hand your Frequent Flier card to the authorities, and walk with dignity to the baggage claim area — then back to the authorities so you can report your lost luggage, secretly believing it has ended up somewhere in Erickland.

This is why, though some marriages are made in heaven, very few ever start in the sky.

Unless your name is Gretchen.

Anytime You Leave No Stone Unturned, You'll Be Fixed Up With A Guy Who's Been Living Under A Rock

I THINK THE PROVERBIAL "FIX-UP" WAS INVENTED TO GIVE WOMEN something they dread more than their annual pap smear.

At least with a pap smear, you know pretty much what you're getting.

Single people never set up blind dates. However, all people currently involved in relationships are required — at least ten or twelve times a year — to throw the names of all the single people they know into an unused crockpot and match them up, out of the goodness of their hearts. These singles don't need any common interests, political viewpoints or food preferences. They don't need to be the same age, race or religion. They don't even have to be potential soulmates. They just have to be single, momentarily

Eat your heart out, Chuck Woolery!

dateless, or guilty of showing up to a couples' event alone (which not only causes an odd attendee number, but also upsets the balance of the person-in-a-relationship's universe). These events trigger the blind-date reflex, and mark the single person as his or her project for life.

What to do when you're the target of a fix-up blind date

You must quickly ask yourself these two serious questions:

1. Have I done anything — anything at all — to offend, upset or anger this person in the past twelve months?

2. Have I ever looked at his or her person-of-choice and been grateful I was single?

If you answered "yes" to either of these questions, immediately lie about JUST having met THE MOST FABULOUS man who may really be THE ONE. This is the only way to get these people off your back.

Although experts agree the odds of actually enjoying a fix-up blind date are equal to winning the lottery, on occasion, we'll give into playing both. It's that "maybe this once" phenomenon that gets us rationalizing every time.

TOP TEN REASONS WE CONVINCE OURSELVES TO ACCEPT BLIND DATES:

10. He's probably no worse than what I'm meeting on my own.

9. At least it's a free dinner.

8. She said he had a *great* personality.

7. It'll give me something to tell my mother.

6. It will give me a reason to shave my legs.

5. It will give me a reason to buy a new outfit.

4. It beats the hell out of watching reruns of *That Girl.*

3. It might be fun.

2. I might like him.

1. He might fall madly in love with me, tell me I'm the most beautiful woman he's ever seen, lavish me with expensive jewelry, and send me five dozen roses "just because."

Even in the age of cynicism, hope springs eternal when it comes to Prince Charming.

So, before you decide to let the next Yenta do her thing, first identify the type of personality who is setting you up. This brief psychological profile can give you clues on what's to come.

The Psychology of the Amateur Matchmaker

Don't say 'yes' to a fix-up blind date until you read this special section.

The "I'm in love so the world should be in love."

This person has recently entered into a whirlwind, head-over-heels relationship, and has now decided that all of her friends should be "coupled," so she never has to spend one waking minute away from her intended. She's the type who draws little hearts over her "i's". She's the type who now tries on bridal gowns during her lunch hour, just four short months after she'd sworn off men for good. She's the type who'll fix you up with a true butthead, and then be amazed that you'd be so picky as to dislike her female-bashing, non-bathing, unemployed redneck friend with an attitude.

The "I'm miserable so everyone else should be miserable, too."

This type, either male or female, is stuck in a marriage so bad, even Oprah wouldn't believe it. Instead of getting divorced, these people adopt the "misery loves company" posture, and insist on trying to marry off all their happily single friends so everyone can suffer together. Their main motivation is creating couples who are willing to go to the movies with them, take vacations with them, and act as on-call babysitters. If they actually fixed you up with a nice guy, it would be purely by accident. If things don't work out after the first date, they'll just tell you you're incapable of commitment and in need of therapy. In reality, they're the ones who need the therapy.

The Obsessive Biological Clock Watcher

This person, usually a parental unit or other older relative, is the self-appointed guardian of your reproductive system. "Use it or lose it" is her philosophy — regardless of whether *you* want children. Because she's seen one too many performances of "Hello Dolly," she's fairly certain her mission in life is to find a father for your nonexistent child. And she'll walk up to complete strangers with your picture to do it. She's on a quest. She's looking for one trait. She's looking for "a boy who is good to his parents." Escape before you're forced to meet him — and the parents he still lives with.

The True Friend With The Best Intentions

This person has her heart in the right place, probably loves you dearly, and is genuinely baffled that a wonderful person like you hasn't found the right man. She's also just as baffled that a wonderful man like her other friend hasn't found the right woman. She's also tired of that vicious attitude you get when you haven't had sex for a while. So, she tries to help. But she's so overwrought with guilt for interfering in your life, and so worried that the whole thing really won't work out, your dear friend insists on being there for the entire meeting. And dominating the conversation. And continuing to dominate the conversation. Then, she'll follow you into the Ladies Room to assure you that there were definitely sparks at the table. Sparks between you and the man who hasn't been able to get a word in edgewise.

This is the one type of blind date that has potential — but only if you lock your friend in the bathroom and manage to get the guy to yourself for a while.

Never Take Out A Classified Ad Unless You're Selling An Isuzu

NO MATTER HOW DETERMINED YOU ARE TO BE THE PROUD RECIPIENT of an FTD bouquet this Valentine's Day…no matter how sick you are of consuming freeze-dried microwave dinners-for-one…and no matter how tired you are of having sole responsibility for your own 3,000-mile oil change, never — I repeat, *NEVER* — call a dating hotline.

Without a doubt, you'll get less than you bargained for.

In a weak moment, it's tempting to call one of these modern-

N/S? 46 yo?
S/DWF? ISO?
VGL? Kds OK?
STD tstd?
hnst? BM?
lo mi??

RENAISSANCE SWF. Luvs wlks mvies art msic msems hmyr wning dndng pking rmnce advntre mrrge. ISO hlthy WM NS/D no kds, 49+ Reply box 954. ☎

STRIKING 24 y.o, 5'9" Claudia Schiffer look-a-like, fun, crvy, sphsti8ted, elgnt & passont party anml. Evrythng u always wnted & more! Box 994. ☎

LARGE & LOVELY Blk, BBW with vluptuous fig, intel, 3 kids, ISO tall attr M, 30-55+ n/s w/intgrty, passion8, glmph, brvdo, prtrg & twklnr w/mjr $$$$. Box 948. ☎

BRAINS/BEAUT., sncr, funluvng, classy, artsy, exotic, ptite N/S sks SWM 30+ 4 outdr activs, trvl, gzbr, rmnce, enzm & luv. N/S/D/R/Y/G/V. Box 993. ☎

CLASSY ENGLISH LADY 30 slm attr sks sucsfl 35+, frnshp/rmnc/mrg? Trvl, hrseback rding & spont-neity.U? N2 ptry, mvies, cookng. Box 943 ☎

SASSY, SULTRY SWF, 5'9"125, seeks sexy, sucsfl. SWM, n/s, 50+ for buddy & beau. Box 949 ☎

HUSBAND WANTED by DWF Dr, 5/6" slndr, VGL, 40s ISO tall, succsfl grnbrd gntlmn 44+ N/S. Box 947.

day singles 911s. Whether they're dating services, Tell-Us-Everything-About-Your-self-In-50-Words-Or-Less ads, high-tech mating services or sub-tech introductory services —they're all really just the same thing. A direct line to 1-900-I-M-Desperate.

REASONS NO WOMAN IN HER RIGHT MIND WOULD EVER CALL 1-900-I-M-DESPERATE

1. You'll meet only social outcasts.

2. No one who calls back will have a full set of teeth.

3. You hate being called a Box.

4. You're dateless, not desperate.

5. At least with a mail-order bride service, you'd be guaranteed meals.

REASONS EVERY SINGLE WOMAN WILL GIVE 1-900-I-M-DESPERATE AT LEAST ONE SHOT

1. A friend will give them your number without telling you.
2. "It can't possibly be worse than meeting men in bars."
3. "If they place an ad, at least I can be sure they can read and write."
4. Maybe you'll meet someone nice.
5. They'll give you the first thirty days *free!*

Before you know it, you'll be armed with a personal ID number, an ad in the local singles rag and a recorded message "describing" yourself to every maniac with a telephone (or a quarter for a pay phone).

In short, everything you need to tell the free world that you can't get a date — or everyone your mother hasn't already informed.

If, after this warning, you still insist on exploring the world of 'In-Search-Of' classifieds, at least learn to translate the ads correctly. The sample ad on the next page, from Box 493H in Dallas, will get you started.

How to dissect a singles ad

Stop writing now!
Do not answer a singles ad
until you read this:

> ATTRACTIVE, FUN-LOVING TEDDY BEAR seeks sensual model type or flight attendant. Bear is very successful, works out, in great shape, tired of bar scene and ready for serious commitment. YOU? Sexy, loyal, friendly, clean. Reply Box 493H

His Ad — Translation

His Ad	Translation
Attractive...	Not as ugly as his brother.
Fun loving...	Won beer guzzling tourney.
Teddy Bear...	"I'm fat and I don't care."
Seeks sensual model type...	Has no grip on reality.
Or flight attendant...	"Can I fly to Vegas for free?"
Is very successful...	Has full tank of gas.
Works out...	Watches mud wrestling.
In great shape...	"So what if I'm fat. You're desperate."
Tired of bar scene...	Gets ignored at bars and must pay for drinks.
Ready for serious commitment...	Wants someone to do dishes.
YOU? Sexy, loyal, friendly...	He just described a puppy with boobs.
Clean.	What on earth has he been going out with?

First impressions turn to depression

How to spot your classified Casanova across a crowded room

Sadly, until we have a female President, there'll never be a lemon law for singles classifieds. More sadly, although you may have answered an ad to get away from the bar scene, you'll more than likely meet this Classified Klutz at a bar for a drink.

Here's what you can expect when Mr. ISO shows up.

THE COTTON-EYED JOE BOB

Has ten-gallon hat and a one-ounce brain. This explains all the air in his head.

THE LEWD WILLIE LOMAN

Heavy-drinking salesman who enters the
bar with his mobile phone and
vibrating beeper. He uses
the phone to call his bookie.
The beeper, well, he just likes the way
it feels.

THE FRIENDLY FEIGNED FOREIGNER

Pretends he is originally from France. Has an accent as fake
as his Rolex. You'd be more attracted to a Conehead.

THE JOHN REVOLTA

Owns more gold medallions
than Mark Spitz. Will spend
the evening telling you
their resale value.

THE LOUIS D. LOSER

Recently divorced and needy. Thinks if he acts pathetic he'll play on your maternal instincts. He doesn't want a date — he wants to remarry ahead of his ex-wife — just for spite. He'll remind you of your cocker spaniel, before house-training.

THE NAME-DROPPING DRIP

He claims he's the reason Clinton got elected, Desert Storm was launched, and Barbra Streisand started touring again. He is the names he knows, although he'll never bother remembering yours. Be glad.

THE TOUCHY-FEELEY CREEPY BILLY

To him, a handshake is a far too impersonal way to greet a total stranger. He says "hello" by groping, "let's go" by patting you on the rear end, and "let's sit here" by grabbing you by the shoulders and turning you toward the table. He should be dating Trigger.

THE WHY BATHE? IT'S JUST THE FIRST DATE

One look at this man and you're certain that a well-meaning friend wrote his singles ad. His mustard-stained shirttail is hanging out, his shirt is unbuttoned, and he carries enough dirt on his body to qualify as a local landfill. He's the one who wants a woman who "loves him for who he is." Unsanitary.

If You're Looking For Mr. Right, Get Over It

I F YOU'RE ONE OF THOSE WOMEN WHO STILL BELIEVES IN THE CONCEPT of Mr. Right...who still dreams of that chivalrous knight in a shining Lincoln Town Car who'll zoom into your life and pick up your dry cleaning without being reminded...who still longs for the prepackaged miracle man who can fulfill all your needs, *and* eat five burritos without belching, I've got three words for you.

Get Over It.

You have as much chance of finding Mr. Right as you do of meeting the Easter Bunny. Why? As this scientific chart proves beyond a shadow of a doubt, both concepts are pure myth.

Peter Cottontail vs. Mr. Right

The Grimm Truth

The Easter Bunny	Mr. Right
Brings joy and happiness.	Ditto.
Encourages you to eat more chocolate.	Ditto.
Is never seen, but rumored to come once a year.	Is never seen.
Has floppy ears and a bushy tail.	Okay, so he's let himself go....

Mr. Right? *NOT!*

This is not to say it's impossible to find a lifelong mate. It's just impossible to find Mr. Right. Your married friends even know this. Just look what they marched down the aisle with:

- Mr. *"Not as Bad as the Other 14,000 Losers I Dated"*
- Mr. *"Sexually Compatible So I Can Overlook Some Flaws"*
- Mr. *"Oh God, What Have I Done"*
- Mr. *"At Least Our Kids Will Be Cute"*
- Mr. *"So What If He's Anal, He Says I Look Good In a Bathing Suit"*
- Mr. *"He Makes Me Laugh"*
- Mr. *"He Makes Me Crazy Only 200 Days A Year"*
- Mr. *"At Least Our Appliances Will Always Work"*
- Mr. *"He's No Prize But Neither Am I"*— or
- Mr. *"I Think He'll Do."*

No matter what they'll tell you, none of your friends married Mr. Right. They married "Mr. Right-For-Me." A guy who didn't fit their original profile. Someone who wasn't what they *thought* they were looking for — but somehow was at the right place at the right time to convince them he was really something they needed.

Kinda like something you find on the sale rack.

How to identify Mr. Right-For-Me using the on-the-spot sale rack technique

1. Is he my size? If not, do I think he'll fit after a couple of months of hard work?
2. Is he a return? If so, can I identify any visible flaws or alimony bankruptcies?
3. Since I'll have to take him "as is," are the flaws well-hidden?
4. Will he go with anything I have?
5. Is he really a bargain, or was the original price overinflated?
6. Do they accept returns?
7. Should I take this one home right now, or should I shop around?
8. Does he only look good on the hanger?
9. Should I take him just because that other woman is eyeing him and I know she'll take him if I put him back?
10. Is this an impulse thing that'll end up hanging in the closet?
11. Is he USA-made, or a cheap import?
12. Is the flaw in the seam, or in the fabric itself?
13. Do I have time to try him on?

> **WARNING:** IF YOU HAVE CLOSETS FULL OF SALE MERCHANDISE YOU NEVER WEAR, ARE A COMPULSIVE SHOPPER, OR HAVE A RELATIVE IN THE GARMENT BUSINESS, IGNORE THIS TECHNIQUE AND MOVE ON TO THE NEXT SECTION.

How to Identify Mr. Right-For-Me

If you really want to be able to identify your Mr.-Right-For-Me when you meet him, here's the secret to being fully prepared:

1. Make a list of all the characteristics you want in your ideal man.

2. Throw away this list.

3. Make a list of all the characteristics you'll want in your ideal man when you're 80 years old in the spinster retirement villa.

Hopefully, your two lists will be different, and you'll no longer include things like, "has his own teeth," "doesn't wear glasses," and "is always in control of his bowel movements."

If your lists are identical, then, at age 80, you'll be looking for a 35-year old man who *still* doesn't exist — and spending your time spouting a mantra of "there are no good men left" to a group of spinsters doing needlepoint on their Depends.

If this kills your idea of a "fantasy man," you're catching on. Although *Cosmo* and Obsession commercials repeatedly tell us differently, Mr. Right-For-You is doomed to be a mere mortal.

Mr. Reality.

The Single Woman's Fantasy-Reality Check

Turn the page to see how well *your* fantasy stacks up against your reality.

She doesn't want sex enough.

He doesn't cuddle. He's cheap. He never puts down the toilet seat. He ogles women at the mall. He doesn't know how to dress. He drives too fast. He can't handle his liquor. He hates my mother. He inhales his food. He belches. He forgot my birthday. I can't tear him away from the TV. He falls asleep right after. He doesn't shave. He doesn't know how to tip. He chews with his mouth open. He leaves his clothes all over the place. He laughs like a hyena. He makes fun of my butt. He brags about his high school glory days. He hogs the blankets. He snores. He

The Single Woman's Fantasy-Reality Check

FANTASY	REALITY
He'll lavish you with gifts for no particular reason.	You've got him confused with Santa Claus, who's already married, anyway.
He'll be tall.	He'll say he's five-foot-ten, although you'll tower over him at five-seven.
He'll look at no other women.	He still thinks Sharon Stone, the swimsuit model in *Sports Illustrated* and the nubile young baby-sitter down the street all want him.
You'll be in his every thought.	He'll spend half his life obsessing about a receding hairline; the other half rehashing the latest game on ESPN.

FANTASY	REALITY
He'll be witty.	He'll still tell knock-knock jokes.
You'll share the same interests.	He'll cancel a romantic evening with you for a tractor pull.
He'll always walk beside you, smother you with kisses, and give you unconditional love.	You've got him confused with the family dog.

Okay, so the guy won't always be a prince — and may rarely be charming. But, then again, you may have a bunion on the foot meant to receive the glass slipper. You see, finding Mr. Right is not the same as finding the perfect man. It's finding an imperfect man who's flaws you start to love.

If you don't believe me, you'd better get back to your pumpkin, Cinderella. You're going to be waiting for a long time.

The Only Reason To Go Dutch Is If You're Dating A Guy Named Hans

E'VE BEEN THROUGH WOMEN'S LIB, THE RISE AND FALL OF THE ERA and the first female to run for Vice-President. We've burned our bras, banned the bomb and even quoted Rosie the Riveter. And because we've come a long way, baby, one thing's become crystal clear: you shouldn't have to pay for a date when *he* invites *you*. That is, until:

1) you're paid an equal salary for the same job
2) men get cellulite
3) men become the primary purchasers of birth control.

This issue has nothing to do with equality. It has everything to do with the cost of equipment women need to prepare for a date.

Cost Comparison
Female vs. Male Dating Prerequisites

WOMEN	MEN
✓ Salon haircut, manicure, pedicure	✓ Remembered to shave
✓ Styling gel, conditioner, hairspray	✓ Plastic comb
✓ Wrinkle cream, eye gel, lip primer	✓ Can of deodorant
✓ Five days at The Diet Center	✓ Skipped lunch
✓ Seven tubes of lipstick	✓ One tube of Chapstick
✓ Designer fragrance	✓ Aftershave received as Christmas gift
✓ Sheer, control-everything pantyhose	✓ Socks he's been wearing since Woodstock I
✓ Electric plaque removal system	✓ One roll of Certs
✓ New outfit, shoes and accessories	✓ Dried undershirt in microwave
✓ Body wrap, leg wax, upper lip bleach	✓ Took shower
TOTAL $2,071.93	TOTAL $6.25

You can now order *a la carte* without guilt.

Every Time You Say "It's Only A Date, How Bad Can It Be?" You'll Get Your Answer Before The Entree

THE PROSPECT OF A FIRST DATE — PARTICULARLY WITH A GUY WHO volunteers to pay for dinner — can seem to be like heaven at first. After all, it's a free meal that won't be at mom's. With an exciting new guy. Isn't that *great*? Won't that be *romantic*?

But think back to other first dinner dates. Memories of slipping into a coma during a three-hour explanation of the principles of CD-ROM. Feeling the overwhelming desire to lay your head in the Caesar salad with the hope that anchovies are viable substi-

...so this morning, I checked to make sure that the pulleys on the blower shaft and the motor was accurately aligned so the belt could ride straight without chafing against the rim of either pulley. And while I was inside the beast, I decided to check the humidifier, and guess what I found?! This HUGE green and yellow fungus. Hell, it even grossed ME out, 'cause it smelled like garbage that was left in the hot sun all day. *Whew!* This crud was really caked in there. I scraped it for over three and a half hours and only stopped because I had to come get you....

tutes for smelling salts. Wishing fervently that someone — *anyone* — would begin choking so you could excuse yourself from this unbearable conversation (or dead silence) to perform the Heimlich Maneuver.

Face it: First dates can be hell.

Ever since I went out with the corporate executive who insisted on unbuttoning his shirt at a restaurant to exhibit a tattoo bigger than my head; or the New Ager who recounted how he brewed tea from bark after severing a branch from a silk ficus; or the strong, silent type who made less conversation than a San Francisco street mime (although he was just as pale), I developed a new dating strategy. First, I NEVER go out to dinner on the first date. It reduces the chance of gas. Second, I've come up with things to do to salvage the evening when the only thing that clicks is the heel of his shoe.

Ways To Amuse Yourself
(and sometimes those around you)

When A First Date
Isn't Clicking

1 Silently add up the number of times he manages to say "I" or "me" in the same sentence.

2 Offer to relieve the busboy during his break. You *may* meet someone else at another table.

3 Pull some dental floss from your purse, make a lasso, and try to rope a breadstick from the next table.

4 Move to another table and see how long it takes your date to notice.

5 Pull a compact from your purse and watch the goings on at the table behind you.

6 Escape to the Ladies Room and kill some time by picking the lock on the tampon machine.

7 Borrow someone's cellular phone. Call a radio therapist.

 MORE...

Ways to amuse yourself when a first date isn't clicking

(continued)

8   If you're dining by candlelight, use the flame to make a spoon ring.

9   Guess what age the man you're with will lose his teeth. Guess at what age he *lost* his personality.

10 See how many dinner rolls you can squeeze into your purse.

11 Crawl under the table and tie his shoelaces together.

12 Play solitaire with the coasters.

13 Fantasize about someone you really like.

THE HAZARD SIGNS OF A DATE FROM HELL

If you've been blessed with wonderful dating experiences up till now (*yeah, right*), you may not recognize a hell date as quickly as you should. These surefire signs are guaranteed to enlighten you:

1. He arrives with a bottle of Mad Dog and a can of Redi-Whip.
2. He slaps you on the butt as a greeting.
3. He begins the evening complaining about how much money he spent on gas to get there.
4. He's not wearing shoes. Or deodorant.
5. He can't pronounce all the items on the menu — and you're at McDonalds.
6. He signals the waiter by doing a pig whistle.
7. He belches more than once.
8. He sighs loudly when you order.
9. He licks the rim of his margarita glass.
10. He licks his fingers.
11. He answers your questions with one-syllable words.
12. He tells you his old girlfriend had a better body.
13. He asks about birth control before he even knows your last name.

This cheap shablis oughta put her in the mood.

It's Just As Easy To Fall In Love With An Older Man As A Younger Man

(unless your name is Cher)

IN DAYS PAST, YOU MAY HAVE INSTINCTIVELY LIMITED YOUR dating universe to men of your own generation, your own decade, or your own graduating year. But now we live in the New Age age, where a world of nips, tucks and dental bonding makes chronology nothing more than a state of mind.

If you're not meeting enough eligible men, why not take advantage of this enlightened era and change your dating standards just a bit — from "within five years of my age" to "between legal age and death." You'll open an amazing world of new opportunities — as long as you know what to expect.

Younger vs. Older

Which is right for *you*?

THE DIFFERENCES

* Puberty.
* Acne.
* Will buy you *Charlie*.
* Can get in for half-price at the movies.
* Thinks Woodstock is Snoopy's friend.
* Thinks older women are sexy.
* Can have sex forever, often with misguided sense of direction.

* Mid-life crisis.
* Dentures.
* May inadvertently *call* you Charlie.
* Can get in for half-price at the movies.
* Thinks Woodstock is purchased at Home Depot.
* Thinks you're young.
* Can have sex. Sometimes.

THE SIMILARITIES

* Both will drive two-seater sports cars. * Both will think you're good in bed.
* Your friends will hate them both.

OEDIPUS OR TYRANNOSAURUS REX — TAKE THE WHAT'S YOUR PREFERENCE QUIZ

Hef & Miss January. Martha Raye and Mark. Cher and whomever. For these folks, age was less of a barrier than a Today Sponge. So which are *you* — an acne attractor, or a "no cane, no gain" kinda woman? If you're not sure, take this quiz. But be honest — no help from the neighborhood kids or local geezers allowed.

1. I think Barney is: a) Andy's assistant sheriff b) the Smurf of the '90s c) a great name for a beagle

2. CD ROM is: a) the capital of Italy b) ancient technology c) a popular country singer

3. AARP is: a) a great place to find cute guys b) how to pronounce Prince's new name c) an annoying dog noise

4. Depends are: a) sexy underwear b) a new birth control device c) a scuba diving mishap

5. I watch *Beverly Hills 90210*: a) Isn't that the one with Jed Clampett? b) I don't watch it — I worship it c) I'm not from California

6. Madonna is: a) someone you see on Christmas cards b) a slut c) I'm not from California

ANSWER KEY
If you answered "a" to four or more questions, start attending Gray Panther meetings.
If you answered "b" to four or more questions, start looking for a mate who reminds you of your kid brother.
If you answered "c" to even one question, you really need to get out a little more often.

THEY SNOOZE, YOU LOSE

You'll also have to be prepared for the sexual differences between older and younger men. For the most part, a simple rule applies: *older men are better, younger men last longer.*

Based on this rule, you might think that the older man is the optimum choice. Not always true. The simple fact is, having sex with an older man means you'll be forced to look at him naked, which may give a younger man the edge. Unless, of course, you are farsighted.

Turbo-charged V-6 pacemaker, my foot!

Granted, there are the sexual similarities, too. Both will fall asleep immediately after orgasm (their own), and neither will call you the next day.

But there are some generational quirks that separate the youngsters from the oldsters. Don't wait till the moment of truth before you learn the facts.

Quirky bedtime habits of each age group

THE YOUNGER MAN

- Has never seen stretch marks and may be a little too inquisitive.
- Will continue to bite until he actually gets milk from your breasts.
- May be the son of someone you dated.
- Gets more turned on by a Mickey Mouse nightshirt than a Victoria's Secret nightgown.
- Might ask why your breasts are unable to hold themselves up.
  - Is sometimes done by the time you get to bed.

THE OLDER MAN

  - Often prefers a good meatloaf to sex, if given the choice (don't).
    - May remove his teeth before foreplay (this can be a good thing).
    - Will often wheeze during orgasm.
    - Actually sags more than you.
    - May buy you dinner beforehand — and actually pay.

Good luck and remember: you're only as old as the man you feel.

If He Doesn't Use A Napkin, He'll Never Use A Condom

WHETHER YOU'VE BEEN ROMANCED WITH A SUMPTUOUS DINNER AT a trendy bistro — or plunged into reality by his habitual choice of restaurants sporting kiddie menus and crayons on the table — you'll never really know a man until he cooks dinner for you. So, before you accept your first home-cooked dinner invitation, it would behoove you to discreetly inspect his kitchen cabinets. That way, you'll know whether to show up with a bottle of Merlot — or a bottle of Maalox.

Cooking skill analysis by kitchen cabinet contents

A little detective work now can save a lot of heartburn later.

ARTHUR SCLEROSIS

CLUES: Paper plates, paper napkins, salt and pepper packets, beenie-weenies, large loaf of white bread, FryBaby, FryDaddy, FryGranDaddy, half-eaten package of HoHos.

ACTION: Refuse invitation even if your cholesterol count is zero. If you really like this guy, suggest take-out from someplace healthier. Like Chubby Burger.

José Heartburn

CLUES: One large Dutch oven, refried beans, ladle, dry taco mix, bulk bag of corn chips, paper bowls, paper towels, piñata.

ACTION: Invest in Beano. You will be eating Frito Pie. Again. And again. And again.

Junk Food Jacques

CLUES: Unopened boxes containing wok, Calphalon cookware, food processor, four-dozen spices you've never heard of, still-shrink-wrapped Betty Crocker recipe cards located next to a huge mound of Jack-in-the-Box wrappers.

ACTION: This man has never used his very expensive oven for anything other than drying sneakers. Eat at your own risk.

BIGFOOT BUBBA

CLUES: Leaning towers of pizza boxes in  the kitchen, paper plates, plastic forks.

ACTION: The only surprise here will be thick or thin crust.

Sir Lancelot

CLUES: Pasta maker, salad spinner, bread baker, spice-of-the-month collection, drying herbs, braid of garlic, packets of yeast.

ACTION: Accept invitation immediately. Double-check gender preference — then call mom and tell her you've met the man you're going to marry.

Tales From The Toaster Oven

And Other Guy-Appliances

Every man who ventures into the wide world of cooking masters one signature appliance — a small electric wonder that he uses every day for every meal, whether the recipe calls for it or not. This appliance is almost never the conventional oven.

The **toaster oven** is the favorite among many males because it's used to pre- pare all foods that "go with" beer — and you never have to clean it. Yet another favorite is the **microwave,** which a typical microwave maniac will use to cook every- thing on the extra-high setting, to give his food that Chernobyl-like texture. Finally, there's the **blender,** the ulti- mate tool of seduction. If you're dating any one of these types of guys, be prepared to dine on one of the following specialties.

TOASTER OVEN MEAT

(The "I'm gonna get lucky tonite special.")

Ingredients

Toaster oven with woodgrain finish

Meat

Salt

Adolph's Meat Tenderizer

A-1 Sauce

Directions

Plug in toaster oven and set on highest possible temperature. Put salt and meat tenderizer on meat, then put meat in oven. (If meat is bigger than oven, fold it over until it fits). Let meat cook through third and fourth quarters of NFL championship game, or until lull in conversation, if during off-season. Turn temperature to 300°. Watch post-game interviews or show date bowling trophies. Remove meat from oven and serve with beer in cans and bread.

The Get Trim Cookbook • 462

Tales From The Toaster Oven

IMPRESSIVE FLAMBÉ MICROWAVE POPCORN FOR TWO

(The "I'm gonna get lucky tonite special.")

Ingredients

High-wattage microwave

Large bag of butter-flavored microwave popcorn

Butter

Salt

Two drippy taper candles

Directions

Place popcorn bag in microwave oven. Cook on extra-high for 19 minutes. Dunk burning bag in sink. Light the candles and hum a Partridge Family medley to drown out the blaring smoke detector. Add enough butter and salt to cover taste of burnt kernels.

The Get Trim Cookbook • 731

Tales From The Microwave

FLOOZIE FRUIT SMOOTHIE

(The "I'm gonna get lucky tonite special".)

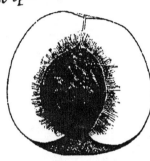

Ingredients

1 blender (with pulverize setting)

4 strawberries

1 week-old banana

4 ounces rum

4 ounces Stoli

4 ounces Everclear

Dash of Mad Dog

Fruit garnish (optional)

Directions

Blend ingredients on high while asking date to put on Barry White CD. Hand her drink and attempt to slip into something more comfortable while she's still conscious but groggy enough to believe that you're Mel Gibson's agent.

The Get Trim Cookbook • 809

Tales From The Blender

Diagnosis of sexual abilities by table manners

Of course, there's more to the mystery of the male than the contents of his kitchen cabinets. You may be privy to his annual income, his life history and his relationship with his mother. But if you really want to know what a man will be like in bed, pay close attention to his table manners. It's a better measure than the size of his hands.

DINING ETIQUETTE	BEDROOM ETIQUETTE
• Fast eater, barely comes up for air, no conversation.	• He's Mr. Hair Trigger.
• Eats slowly, never finishes anything.	• Will fall asleep during foreplay, call it "the best he's ever had" — *and mean it.*
• Talks with mouth full.	• Will never stop talking. May even scream out own name.
• Leaves table immediately after finishing.	• You won't see him in the morning.
• Never uses a napkin.	• Will never use condom.
• Gets more food on clothing than in his mouth.	• Will miss the target completely.
• Likes to linger over coffee.	• *IS* the marrying kind.

RULE № 18

Everyone Should Carry Papers

I'T'S TRUE, LIFE WAS MORE ROMANTIC IN OUR YOUNGER DAYS — back when we weren't required to boil our dates before shaking their hands. Times have certainly changed.

We whizzed right past that era of spontaneity into the time of the Trojan woman. Now, all our married friends are frenetically flinging cartons of condoms in our direction, filled with enough multicolored creations to bring zero-population growth to many Third World countries. There's not a single person alive who has the time or energy to make use of all these rubber wonders before their expiration dates. Very few of us can use up an entire carton of eggs!

I, for one, appreciate my friends' concern. But I'm running out of storage space. Unused condoms are overtaking my glove compartment, my trunk, and now outnumber the dust balls under my bed. They line the bottom of my purse, pop out of my bathroom drawers and fill up wardrobe-sized boxes in my garage labeled "Christmas." Yet, although I'm well-armed, I *still* don't feel totally safe.

This is why everyone should be forced to carry papers.

I know, it sounds a little restrictive. But sometimes a clean bill of health can spark an impetuous moment. It's tough having a Dr. Zhivago-type fantasy with a tall, handsome stranger when you're wondering why he's had reason to use up his medical deductible so early in the year. If we all carried papers, we'd no longer be gifted with trendy condom jewelry, condom mobiles, condom lamp shades and cutesy condom repair kits. Insurance rates would plummet. And sex would be safer once again.

We would file our papers once a year, together with our income tax returns. Questionable forms would be subject to an audit by the Surgeon General. Or Helen Gurley Brown. And the form would look like this.

Should I even bother to tell them about the one-nighter with that cleaning lady who didn't speak English??

Does he qualify for the Short Form?

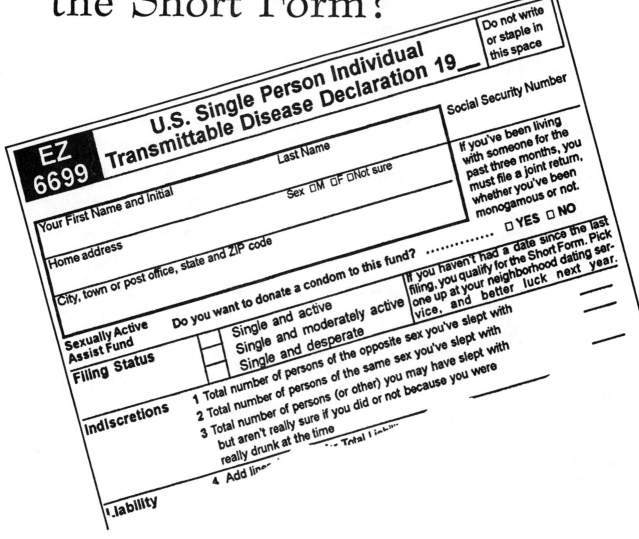

U.S. Single Person Individual
Transmittable Disease Declaration 19__

Do not write or staple in this space

EZ 6699

Last Name

Your First Name and Initial

Sex □M □F □Not sure

Social Security Number

If you've been living with someone for the past three months, you must file a joint return, whether you've been monogamous or not.

□ YES □ NO

Home address

City, town or post office, state and ZIP code

Do you want to donate a condom to this fund? ....

If you haven't had a date since the last filing, you qualify for the Short Form. Pick one up at your neighborhood dating service, and better luck next year.

Sexually Active Assist Fund

Filing Status

Single and active
Single and moderately active
Single and desperate

Indiscretions

1 Total number of persons of the opposite sex you've slept with
2 Total number of persons of the same sex you've slept with
3 Total number of persons (or other) you may have slept with but aren't really sure if you did or not because you were really drunk at the time

4 Add lines ... Total Liability

Liability

...id or not because you...

... really -

... really drunk at the time

really drunk at the time

4 Add lines 1,2 and 3 for Total Liability Earned

5 Total number of times condoms were used successfully

6 Subtract lines 5 from 4

Liability

If Item 6 is more than zero, you are required to complete Schedule C, listing all the persons (and other) you've slept with by name and rating. They will be audited for disease and rating (that's what you get for not using a condom).

If you've slept with two or more people at one time, you must complete Schedule D and enclose photos.

Adjustments
Check if

☐ you've slept with someone 65 or older   ☐ you've slept with a relative
☐ you've slept with someone who's young enough that their parents still
   claim them as a dependent

Credits

☐ Credit for having dinner with date first   ☐ Credit for calling the next day
☐ Credit for being the primary purchaser of condoms
☐ Credit for knowing the name of the last few people you've slept with

Commitment
State the number
of times you:

1. Slept with someone because you hoped for a meaningful relationship
2. Slept with someone because they were cute
3. Slept with someone for no apparent reason
4. Slept with someone because they accepted

Add lines 2-4. Subtract from line 1

If this total is 2 or above, your medical Okay-By-Me badge and notarized certificate will be forwarded to you within 30 days. If this number was 0 or in the negative range, you've had quite enough. The auditor will appear at your condo shortly.

	Date	Your Occupation
		Check if self-employed
Your signature	Date	
Your preparer's signature		

Sign Here

Under penalties of perjury, I declare that I have examined this return and accompanying schedules and doctors' notes, and to the best of my knowledge and belief, they are true, correct and complete.

Your Sexual Peak Will Occur At The Exact Moment Gravity Takes Control Of Your Rear End

THE CONCEPT OF A WOMAN'S SEXUAL PEAK IS NOT A MYTH. FAR from it. It's a rite of passage filled with passion, steaming sexual creativity and a craving that surpasses that for Peanut M&Ms. And it will always occur at a time when you're:

a) not in a relationship;

b) have no potential for a relationship;

c) have resorted to taking your best friend's cousin to a wedding, just so you'll have someone under the age of 90 to dance with.

If this Bionic-woman-like libido-gone-unfulfilled isn't frustrating enough, another strange phenomenon will take place simultaneously. You'll begin to get bruises — large black-and-blue marks — on the back of your knees and down your calves. Bruises caused by a butt that's succumbed, practically overnight, to Newton's Law of Gravity — and is now slamming against the flipside of your anatomy whenever you walk faster than your great grandmother.

BUTT WAIT... THERE'S MORE!

Granted, it's not the end of the world. On the positive side, it's an airtight medical excuse for giving up high-impact aerobics. It also enhances your balance by lowering your center of gravity. And the dangling flesh adds valuable insulation for protection during those harsh winter months.

Eventually, the remainder of your body will breathe a sigh of relief and start diving downward as well — making you immediately attractive to shorter men and drunks lying face-up on the street.

Like it or not, you may have already entered your gravity-prone years. The checklist on the next page will tell you for sure.

The at-home gravity checklist

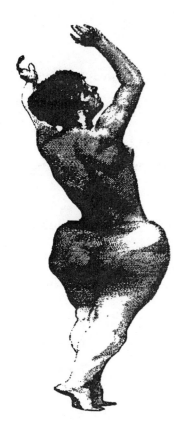

☑ Does your rear end cover the top of your thigh-high boots? Knee-high boots? Ankle boots?

☑ When you flap your arms, do you become airborne?

☑ Does your face now hang like Deputy Dawg's?

☑ When you remove your pantyhose, does the flesh form around your feet like ankle weights?

☑ When you remove your bra, do you hear a thud on the ground in front of you? Does the same noise come from behind when you remove your jeans?

☑ Has it been more than a year since you've been able to see anything more than a top view of your nipples?

☑ If you lie down on the bed when you put on your jeans, do you get up looking like the Hunchback of Notre Dame?

☑ If you turn and look behind you quickly, does it take ten minutes or more before the rest of you stops moving?

☑ Has your body started to look less like Linda Hamilton's and more like Alexander Hamilton's?

If you answered "yes" to five or more of these questions, you've entered the gravity-prone zone. If you answered *"oh, yes!"*

to all of these questions, you're now the Isaac Newton poster child. Have yourself an apple.

SEX WITH A LOWER CENTER OF GRAVITY

As much as you're dripping with sexual drive and oozing with ultra-orgasmic potential, the other half of the equation says that men your age will rarely be able to keep up with you. Oh, they'll try. They'll try so hard they'll fall asleep. Typically, four-and-one-half hours before you're through.

To compound this cruel trick of nature, the gravity issue actually makes sex a little more dangerous. You now run the risk of accidentally blinding yourself with your own chest by just rolling into position. Worse yet, you can suffocate your partner with a butt that expands faster than an automobile airbag upon impact.

You may try to exercise, lift weights or spend 40 hours a week doing the "Buns of Steel" video, but, at best, you'll be able to raise only six percent of your rear no more than an inch-and-a-half, creating more of a bowl of Jello than a bun of steel. This is an excellent time to learn a new trick about sex: how to get intimate without turning around.

Top (10) ways to get intimate without turning around

10 *Always* race your partner to the bedroom — and *always* let him win.

9 Learn to strike seductive poses that involve leaning against walls, large-screen TVs, and sitting in chests of drawers.

8 Carry a large can of black-matte paint and insist on spraying any ceiling mirror you encounter.

7 In extreme cases, you can spray the black-matte paint on your rear end, since black makes everything look smaller.

6 Have sex outdoors every opportunity you can. Just dig a hole in the sand and/or dirt and submerge yourself until you have the body of Christie Brinkley.

5 If you have to leave the room while naked, divert his attention

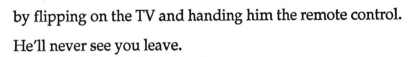

by flipping on the TV and handing him the remote control. He'll never see you leave.

4 Insist on waltzing to wherever you plan to have sex. The woman always moves backwards.

3 Blindfold your partner and insist he leave it on before, during and after sex.

2 Tell him you want to gaze into his eyes (or wherever) for as long as possible. This will give you an excuse for always backing out of the room.

1 If you must remove your control-top, heavy-support pantyhose while he's in the room, make sure you do it at the exact moment your partner is unzipping his pants. He'll proudly think the inevitable thud of falling flesh is caused by some part of *his* anatomy.

Men are gullible that way.

Greeting Cards Should Be Sold At Home Depot

OMETIMES I LONG FOR THE DAYS OF ROBERT BROWNING — where long, lush love letters were the order of the day. When it was worth the four-month Pony Express wait for the passionate prose written by all those Messrs. Right-For-Me of yore.

Alas, those days are gone forever.

Now, we're lucky enough if we have a Mr. Right-For-Me who pays his bills on time, without expecting him to put something in the mail that isn't due 30 days net.

Roses are red.........?
How do I love thee......?.
Once upon a time.......?
Oooohhh baby I love
yer way........

Hallmark and others have tried to bridge the gap. Card stores are filled with racks upon racks of prepackaged love notes — with glorious color and flowery graphics — just waiting for the man who truly cares enough to send the very best.

This almost never happens. Because, to most men, entering a Hallmark store is pretty much the equivalent of touching a box of tampons. It's gross. It's unnecessary. It's scary. They're afraid that the smell of potpourri will give them the dry heaves. That the choices will be overwhelming. And that there's simply too much reading involved. Then, of course, they'll have to buy a stamp. All of which will make you think they're far more committed than they actually are. So they go bowling with the boys, instead.

This is why greeting cards should be sold at Home Depot. If a man is going to make an impulse buy, this is where it's going to happen. The smell of sawdust puts him in a romantic mood to begin with. The hum of power tools brings out the primal instinct. If the greeting cards were artfully positioned somewhere between the jigsaws and the wing nuts, men might be inclined to make a purchase — particularly if they saw other manly handymen doing the same.

What's in the card?

What women want
greeting cards to say
∨

What men want
greeting cards to say
∨

Somewhere in the evolutionary process, the Robert Browning hormone must have undergone some strange mutation. But until Hallmark gets a clue, the most romantic note any of us can hope to receive from any male will begin with "Dear Occupant."

What women are ready to settle for in a greeting card

What men end up purchasing

If greeting card companies were thinking, they could increase their sales *and* bring bliss to the women of America just by finding new outlets for the illusive Hallmark special. Places men go. Places men love. Places without the dreaded scent of potpourri.

Hallmark, if you're listening, here are my suggestions.

PRIME LOCATIONS FOR IMPULSE GREETING CARD PURCHASES BY MEN

1. By the Fritos at 7-Eleven.
2. In the Craftsman Tool department at Sears.
3. At stadium souvenir shops.
4. By the jock straps in sporting goods stores.
5. In the cellular phone section at Circuit City.
6. At the beer stand at golf tournaments.
7. Between the gas pumps.
8. In the Blockbuster Video *Three Stooges* section.
9. At the neighborhood bar.
10. In the seatpocket of every major airline.
11. At the checkout counter of Denny's.
12. In the G-string of Sheila the Reptile Dancer at the Hubba-Hubba Au Go-Go.

If He Says He Needs Space, Suggest He Move To Utah

OKAY, SO YOU THINK YOU KNOW THE GUY. THE GUY WHO ASKED you if you wanted children when you weren't even sure if you wanted dessert. The man who was sure — on the first date — that you were the one, when you were sure he was nothing but one of many. In time, you discovered he was right. Maybe even Mr. Right-For-Me.

And just when he got you speaking the language of love, he suddenly switched over to communicating with you in code. The Secret Code of Hazy Commitment — a time-tested method to preserve bachelorhood. Statements that can mean anything, depending on: a) the man's level of fear at the time he says them; b) the incidence of new, nubile female neighbors, co-workers or bartenders entering his universe; and, c) which one of his beer buddies he's last talked to.

I need to see other people.

Do you know the song, "Freebird?"

I feel trapped.

I need my space

Maybe we should slow this down.

Give me time.

It's too soon to get serious.

I'M CONSIDERING TAKING A JOB IN POCATELLO.

Maybe it's time for my boot-heels to be wanderin.'

IT'S NOT YOU... IT'S ME.

I never said this was exclusive.

The Official Male Commitment Code pocket translator

SECRET CODE	POSSIBLE TRANSLATIONS
"I need my space."	1. "You're standing on my foot." 2. "I'm thinking of becoming an astronaut." 3. "I'm getting so serious about you I'm thinking of wearing a tux, but my friend Bob told me not to jump in too soon."
"I need to see other people."	1. "I made an appointment to have my eyes examined." 2. "A twenty-year-old flight attendant was nice to me, so I'd like to string you along while I can see if I'm capable of attracting something better." 3. "I'm getting so serious about you I'm thinking of renting a tux, but my friend Bob told me not to jump in too soon."
"I feel trapped."	1. "Untie me — these handcuffs are cutting off my circulation." 2. "I'm having flashbacks of being locked in an airplane bathroom." 3. "I'm so serious about you that I have the urge to buy a tux, but my friend Bob has a lousy marriage and says you'll soon have me in your trap, too."

"It's too soon to get serious."

1. "I can't afford a set of tires, much less a ring."
2. "I haven't gone steady since junior high and that never panned out, either."
3. "I'm so serious about you that I have the urge to get a tux, but my friend Bob told me it was too soon to get serious unless I want to live with a noose around my neck for the rest of my natural existence."

"Give me time."

1. "My watch has stopped ."
2. "I'm not as young as I used to be and it takes longer for all the parts to work."
3. "My friend Bob said I should date every woman in the free world before I decide to make a commitment to you."

If the commitment code was the only strange communication technique used by this guy, you could easily solve all your problems by getting rid of Bob. Unfortunately, life's not that easy. Some of the most difficult things to translate are the things a guy *doesn't* say. This practice, known as Auditory Zen, is evident in good and bad relationships, first dates, and twenty-year marriages.

Auditory Zen enables a man to read the paper, memorize batting averages and ponder junk bonds while appearing to hang on your every word. However, through intense mind control, he can block out large portions of your conversation while subconsciously absorbing key phrases for future use. These phrases can then be repeated, either indignantly — or accompanied by deep sighing — when he is "wrongly" accused of not paying attention to you.

To be totally effective, Auditory Zen should be combined with a series of head aerobics. Nodding, cocking the head to the right or left and an occasional chin quiver all enhance the illusion. Simple vocal constrictions, creating "hmmmm" and "uh-huh" sounds are not only designed to ensure you that he is fascinated with everything you have to say, but gives him full freedom to enjoy reruns of Mayberry RFD over your right shoulder.

THE AUDITORY "DEAD ZONE"

The true Auditory Zen Master has yet another trick up his larynx: the Auditory "Dead Zone." If you're unfamiliar with this technique, it's an advanced state of silence where your Mr. Right-For-

Me suddenly appears glassy-eyed and semi-comatose. In reality, it's a survival method used when he's caught in a lie, proven wrong in an argument, or invited to a wedding.

WHY MEN USE ADVANCED SILENCE TECHNIQUES

1. Don't know answer.
2. Forgot the question.
3. Forgot your name.
4. You are making a valid point.
5. Potential confrontation.

WHAT YOU CAN DO WHEN FACED WITH AN ADVANCED SILENCE EMERGENCY

Sometimes works:

1. Threaten to take a lover. Someone who speaks.
2. Slowly say *"Vee haf vays uf maykeeng you tok!"* while heating up the curling iron.
3. Threaten to call his mother for advice.

Never works:

1. Reason.
2. Attempting a silence stand-off.
3. Sticking out your tongue.

Always works:

1. Hide the TV remote.

If He's Not Shaving After The First Year, Neither Should You

A "COMFORTABLE RELATIONSHIP." SOMETHING WITH LONG-TERM potential. That's what we're going for, right?

To single women, dating the same guy for a year means we begin to think about him as a life partner. We're free to express our hopes, dreams and fears without insecurity. We develop a bond that transcends space and time.

To a man, a yearlong relationship means he no longer has to change his underwear on a regular basis.

"The Thrill Is Gone" Comparison Chart

DURING THE FIRST MONTH, HE...	AFTER THE FIRST YEAR, HE...
• Wears your favorite aftershave.	• Reeks of St. Pauli Girl.
• Worries his five o'clock shadow will give you razor burn.	• Doesn't shave on weekends.
• Wears starched shirts at your house.	• Wears no shirt.
• Introduces you to his friends.	• Hangs out solo with his buddies.
• Sends flowers for no reason.	• Sees no reason to send flowers.
• Buys new underwear.	• Still wears same stretched-out briefs he bought five years ago.

Shortly after the first date.

DURING THE FIRST MONTH, HE...	AFTER THE FIRST YEAR, HE...
• Buys you Godiva chocolates.	• Tells you you've gained weight.
• Plans romantic dates.	• Mumbles "what's for dinner?"
• Cleans his car before each date.	• Prefers to drive *your* car.
• Sends you love notes.	• Leaves you grocery lists.
• Calls you four times a day.	• Calls if his car breaks down.
• Serves dinner by candlelight.	• Eats dinner in front of the TV.
• Takes you on moonlit strolls.	• Falls asleep on the couch.
• Wants to meet your family.	• Wants to watch reruns of the *Addams Family.*
• Prefers sex to anything.	• Sex, nap, food, sports and TV are pretty much toss-ups.
• Falls asleep after sex.	• Falls asleep before sex.

z

Shortly after the first year.

THE "HEAT 'EM UP" AFTER ONE YEAR DEFENSE GUIDE*

You, on the other hand — unaware of the testosterone time bomb that detonates in a male after 365 days with the same woman — attempt to rekindle the flame. You worry that he no longer finds you attractive, has found another woman, or is having a mid-life crisis. None of these things is true. He's just secure enough in the relationship to show you what he really is. A slug.

YOU...	HE...
Dance naked on top of the TV.	Voices concern about the reception.
Have a spree at Victoria's Secret.	Dozes off before you get the teddy snapped.
Plan a romantic picnic.	Complains of pollen count.
Write him a seductive note.	Uses the back of it to record mileage.
Get a new haircut, lose five pounds, buy a new outfit.	Says you look tired.
Buy a billboard proclaiming your love for him.	Discovers an alternate route to work.
Ask him why he doesn't love you anymore.	Looks baffled and dozes off.

---

* Rarely works

You Have Met The Enemy, And It Is His "Ex-*Life*"

F YOU'RE IN THAT "SOMEWHERE-BETWEEN-THIRTY-AND-CAN-LEGALLY-withdraw-from-your-IRA-without-penalty" age, you've been around long enough to know that good perfume comes in small bottles, great wine requires a corkscrew, and no one gets thin thighs in thirty days. You consider yourself fairly well planted in reality. But if you still think you're going to find a well-dressed, witty, delightful man with no ex-wife, no joint custody, no alimony and no ex-in-laws who still tell him that he "never gave the marriage a chance," it's time to grow up. You're as delusionary as a man who thinks he's going to marry a virgin.

So, prepare yourself to date a man who's divorced, whose past is still a part of his present, and whose priorities vary with the school lunch menu. The only thing you'll know for sure is that you'll never be Number One on the list. Here's why:

THE NEWLY DIVORCED MAN'S GUILT-RIDDEN PRIORITY LIST

1. His children
2. His dog
3. His home (that's the one he *used to* live in)
4. "Couple" friends left over from marriage
5. Income tax filing options
6. Leaky faucet at house he used to live in
7. Overdue bills
8. Heartbroken parents
9. Heartbroken in-laws
10. $150/hour therapist
11. Fellow divorcees in recommended support group
12. Vaccination day at school
13. Cholesterol screening results
14. Vehicle maintenance and cleaning

15. Stock portfolio losses

16. Water aerobics (part of the "new" him)

17. Dollar Day at McDonalds

18. Personal space

19. Personal time

20. Commiserating with buddies about alimony

21. Commiserating with buddies about playoffs

22. Semi-annual Roto-Rooter check at old house

23. *You*

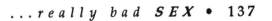

During Peewee football, T-ball, soccer, family reunions or leap years, you will fall even lower on the list. In fact, you have a better chance of giving birth to an alien wolfboy or marrying Elvis than making that vertical climb.

Unless, of course, you kidnap his dog.

THE FAMILY TIES THAT GAG

One way to TRY to move up on his priority list is to involve yourself in divorced father-kid weekend activities. Then you can discover the dynamics of Putt-Putt golf, advance to Grand Master in Nintendo, and pop enough Drama-mine to get you through the inevitable trip down the 78-story water slide without incident.

Yet nothing — but *nothing* — will prepare you for your first meeting with his children. Just get ready for a conversation that will go something like this:

HIM: "Kids, this is (*your name here*)."

YOU: "Hi!"

KIDS: "YOU'RE NOT MY MOTHER."

(Followed by dead silence through a four-hour Monster Truck rally, a two-scoop stop at Baskin-Robbins and a 20-minute romp through The Dollar Store.)

Even if you owned Disneyland,

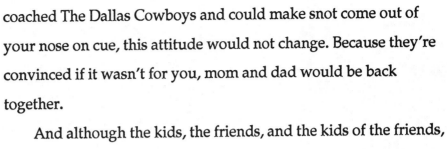

coached The Dallas Cowboys and could make snot come out of your nose on cue, this attitude would not change. Because they're convinced if it wasn't for you, mom and dad would be back together.

And although the kids, the friends, and the kids of the friends, won't accept you because you're *nothing* like mom, their father is terribly afraid that you are indeed *exactly* like his ex-wife.

Should you be so bold as to display one similarity to this woman — be it a preference for the same political party or the ownership of two ovaries — he'll convince himself that you're her evil twin, and that the entire relationship will soon reek of divorcee déjà vu. Here's why:

The new girlfriend/ ex-wife comparison
As interpreted by the male mind

YOU...	HE THINKS...
• Own a TV.	• You'll sell his guitar in a garage sale.
• Have his ex's blood type.	• You'll make him eat carrots.
• Have his ex's middle name.	• You'll make fun of his bald spot.
• Like to cook.	• You won't let him eat in the car.
• Took ballet as a child.	• You'll start quoting Oprah.
• Just like his ex, also carry a purse.	• You only want his money.
• Just like his ex, see a gyno once a year for an exam.	• You were sent to make his life a living hell for not sticking to the lousy marriage he was in.

TOP TEN THINGS TO DO WHILE WAITING FOR A DIVORCEE-IN-DOUBT

When all else fails, why not take advantage of all the free time you have to learn some valuable skills:

10 Learn a foreign language — like Italian or West Texan.

9 Find a tanning gel that doesn't streak.

8 Design a health plan that can pass both Houses of Congress.

7 Learn the guitar, join a grunge band, and start touring.

6 Campaign for handicapped parking for the emotionally crippled.

5 Buy a puppy, breed her, and make a mint off the litters.

4 Learn the metric system once and for all.

3 Run away with a circus.

2 Call your mother.

1 Find a man who has time — and makes time — to spend with you.

Mr. Wrong Wants To Hitch You & Mr. Right Wants To Ditch You

I'T'S A FUNNY THING ABOUT A RELATIONSHIP. AS SOON AS YOU DECIDE that it's over, it's done, that it has the disaster potential to make the last days of Pompeii look like a greasefire, he will decide you're his lifelong companion, plan a major jewelry purchase and start naming your unborn kids. Typically, this occurs on the same day you've set aside to let him down easy.

This presents a problem.

Because, although the handwriting on the wall may warn "the end is near," he sees a long-term future. And although every date becomes more of a fight for conversation, an exercise in boredom, and a mental interrogation of "why the heck am I wasting my time here?" — *he's* fallen in love. In love with the hideous woman who's about to dump him. A process that, if you're a relatively nice woman like me, goes in phases.

PHASE ONE — "I KNOW...I'LL MAKE IT *HIS* IDEA!"

- ◆ Start displaying every horrible habit you can dredge up. Take up smoking for the short-term — cigars if you have to.
- ◆ Introduce him to every single female you know, in hopes that he'll like one of them better than you.
- ◆ Start wearing flannel nightgowns, waist-high cotton underwear, support hose, and a limited amount of makeup in unflattering colors.
- ◆ Start claiming financial failure, ties to the mob or the sudden urge for long-term celibacy.
- ◆ Clip out-of-state job opportunities in his chosen profession, and encourage him to apply.
- ◆ Insist he spend more time with your parents, or at the mall.

His reaction: All of these actions typically make him love you more. This makes you feel even more guilty. Which is why you start paying for dinner. Or consider marrying him anyway, just to avoid hurting his feelings. *Don't.*

PHASE TWO: "He'll agree with me once I explain it to him clearly."

♦ Tell him you "need to talk."

♦ Cook his favorite meal, buy his favorite wine, wear his favorite color, but refuse to shave your legs.

♦ Explain that you're not good enough for him.

♦ Highlight the quirks of your personality that don't lend themselves to long-term commitment.

♦ Encourage him to find the right woman — that special woman — who has all the love and devotion a true catch like him deserves. Then compliment his tie.

His reaction: He smiles and says "I thought I found the right woman" (which gives you hope this phase is working). He proceeds with, "And now I'm sure of it!" Then he asks if you can name your first child Zachary Michael, after his great-grandfather, who would have loved you as much as he does. You smile politely and start downing shots.

PHASE THREE: "NO MATTER HOW HARD IT IS, I'M GOING TO BE BLATANTLY HONEST."

♦ Tell him you *really* need to talk.

♦ Meet him at a public place, in case he gets out-of-hand.

♦ Tell him you don't think the relationship is working, list 17 or more reasons, and give him specific examples of what you need from a relationship that he is not providing.

♦ Let him know you're doing him a favor for telling him honestly, and that, years from now, when he's found his perfect lifemate, he'll thank you for it.

♦ Thank him for (*fill in the time frame*) of his time and company.

♦ Give him a hug and tell him "I'll always remember you."

His reaction: He says "what are you talking about, we don't have any problems. And if we do, I'm sure we can work them out." Then he asks you out for the following night.

PHASE FOUR: "IF I DON'T DUMP THIS MAN, I'M GOING TO END UP IN THE BETTY FORD CLINIC."

- Drive to his house unannounced.
- Tell him that he's a sorry excuse for a human being and that you'd rather kiss a dead animal than have any physical contact with him ever again.
- Tell him that he's so boring that he makes your junior high civics teacher look like Mr. Charisma.
- Tell him you want out of the relationship, and want out now.
- Hand him a sack of everything he ever gave you, a Baggie of torn photographs and a typewritten list of all the things he did to exasperate you during the course of the relationship.
- Make a flourishing exit, drive away, and don't look back.

His reaction: He'll call the next day and ask if you're over the PMS yet.

Or Mr. Right will want to ditch you

For every Mr. Wrong you've ever dumped there's a potential pay-back further on down the road. Just when you think you've found the man you want to spend the rest of your life with...the man who fulfills your wishes and dreams...the man you're willing to cook for, baby-sit for, compromise for, lay down your life for... the man you think is Mr. Right — he will dump you flat.

Men don't have multiple dumping phases. Being the creatures of action they are, they have only two methods of dumping:

1. Stop calling for no apparent reason.

2. Leave a message on your answering machine saying that they're either going back to the woman they were with before you, or to a new woman who is everything you aren't. "Hey," they say, "I know you'll be okay."

No explanation. No free dinner. No niceties. Just an answering machine tape that you'll play over and over again, trying to read between the lines to find the magic answer to the word *"why?"*

If you have the urge to call and ask him just that, I can save you the trouble. All male dumpers say the same thing. "It's just the way it is." Like this is a big help. A typical female will then

So, I..er...guess we...ah... won't be seeing too much of each other from now on because I...ah... met this...er...wonderful flight attendant named Gretchen and I guess I'll be in Paris with her by the time you get this message but...ah...hey, I know you'll be okay.

assess the situation, ponder the big picture, and come to the conclusion that if she'd have only spent more time on the Stairmaster, this never would have happened.

OUT-OF-THE-DUMPS STRATEGIES FOR THE WOMAN WHO'S BEEN DUMPED BY MR. RIGHT

1. Lie down on the couch with every picture you have of this man.

2. Play one of the following songs on auto-repeat for the next five hours:

➤ *You Can't Take That Away From Me* by Barbra Streisand

➤ *Someday* by Mariah Carey

➤ *I Will Survive* by Irene Cara

➤ *Heart of the Matter* by Don Henley

➤ *I Can't Make You Love Me If You Don't* by Bonnie Raitt

➤ *I Think I Love You* by the Partridge Family

➤ *These Boots Are Made For Walking* by Nancy Sinatra

➤ *Am I Blue?* by Fanny Brice

➤ *Glad Rags and Handbags* by Rod Stewart

➤ *What I Did For Love* by the original cast of *A Chorus Line*

3. Rip the pictures into tiny little pieces. Tear out and keep any flattering photos of you.

4 Write a complimentary letter to Lorena Bobbitt.

5. Pray his next girlfriend discovers she's gay.

6. Eat something that originally belonged to Sara Lee.

7. Call a few friends and coerce them into egging his house.

8. Laugh about the eggs.

9. Cry about the situation.

10. Wonder what's wrong with you.

11. Really wonder what's wrong with him.

12. Call more friends.

13. Erase the answering machine tape.

14. Egg his house yourself. It's not really productive, but it will make you feel better.

15. Repeat 1 through 14 until you meet the next Mr. Right. The real Mr. Right. The non-butthead version.

This is why I think we all should be equipped with traffic signals on our foreheads, so we can really see when a relationship is going somewhere. Or nowhere.

When It Comes To Understanding Women, Men Have No Clue

HE MAY BE A ROCKET SCIENTIST — A MULTI-LINGUAL GENIUS WHO scores high at both Trivial Pursuit and chess. He may enrapture you with dinner conversation on nuclear physics, Einstein's theories and Renaissance art. But the instant the topic turns to women, you can almost see his giant IQ take a vertical nose-dive — transforming your Dr. Science into Barney Fife.

He can't help it. He's spent a lifetime being taught about women by the traditional Testosterone Triple Threat. The Triad of Terror. The Multiplex of Misinformation: Dad. *Playboy.* And the Boy Scouts of America.

With these influences, it's no wonder the poor boy's confused.

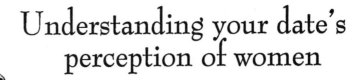

Understanding your date's perception of women

Perception   Anyone who doesn't have a beard shouldn't spend so much time in the bathroom.

Reality   *Just try using an Epilady, buddy.*

Perception   Women grow irritable once a month.

Reality   *Women grow irritable MORE than once a month.*

Perception   Women shop too much.

Reality   *At least I didn't order a lifetime supply of that bald-spot spray.*

Perception   Women are offended when a man pays for dinner.

Reality   *After an evening with you, you should pay for dinner and leave me a big tip for the aggravation.*

Perception   Women are offended if you don't make a move on them on the first date.

Reality   *You were really gross in the sitting position. What makes you think....*

Perception	Women want men smarter than they are.
Reality	*We're more realistic than that.*
Perception	Women tell intimate life secrets to strangers in the Ladies Room.
Reality	*No, we just laugh about you.*
Perception	No woman can actually fall into the toilet.
Reality	*Okay. This one's true.*

THE MOTHER FACTOR

The most surprising influence on this twisted guy-think comes from a source you might not suspect: his mother — the female-of-origination. The woman who nurtured him. Guided him. Raised him.

Today, he may think he's a grown-up, but in truth, he's never far away from those classic maternal mantras that play like Springsteen CDs in the depths of his brain. Here are a few choice examples.

Incredible Oedipals

How guys interpret what their mothers
drummed into their heads

Memorable Maternal Quote	Subconscious Reaction
"You were in diapers till you were 11."	Always leave the toilet seat up.
"Listen when I'm talking to you."	Turn on the TV.
"Children are starving in Africa."	Secretly feed your vegetables to the dog.
"Just wait till *you* have children."	Always use birth control.
"You'll thank me for this later."	Put off saying thanks.
"If you're smart, you'll marry a woman who's just like me."	Never get married.

THE HEART OF THE MALE BELIEF SYSTEM

Okay, so it's easy to see why men don't understand women. But, what's *our* excuse? We can try logic. We can try analysis. But we'll never understand men until we comprehend the driving force of the male being. The very root of his existence.

The Male Ego.

I used to think the ego was located somewhere inside the TV remote control, which would explain the attachment. Or near the place guys stick their hands when they fall asleep on the couch. Or in the stomach, which would account for its amazing growth throughout the life of a man and during the consumption of beer.

Wherever it is, it's the heart of a male belief system that's too bizarre for words.

The rules of male ego development

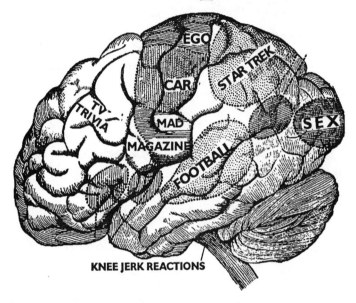

- Men never need directions. They simply know which way to go.
- Men never need instructions. They assemble by instinct.
- Men never age. Just look at Dick Clark.
- Men are immortal. Just look at Elvis.

THE FIVE WARNING SIGNS OF A BRUISED MALE EGO

Because of its size, the male ego makes an easy target, and can be easily injured. Watch for these warning signs:

1. Excessive silence, even during major sporting events.

2. Assorted pouting, including, but not limited to: speeding, running red lights, wandering aimlessly from room to room, assuming the fetal position and sculpting his mashed potatoes into little animal shapes.

3. A sudden absorption in Gilligan and Skipper as they attempt to solve Ginger's problem.

4. Audible whining and sighing.

5. Finding his trophy for "closest to the hole" dumped in trash.

Take heart. The male ego is so highly developed, its ability to recover is truly remarkable. In fact, it usually heals on its own within a matter of minutes. But, if dinner reservation time is fast approaching and you want to speed up the recovery process, just follow the simple procedures on the next page and get on with the evening in comfort.

Ego Rescue
911 Hotline Recovery Tips
for the Affected Female

1 Tell him last night was *wonderful*, unless, of course, you were out of town.

2 Tell him he reminds you of Fabio, but with verbal skills.

3 Compliment any body part that protrudes.

4 Perform a dramatic reading of his yearbook credentials.

5 Tell him you get the urge to take off your clothes when he smiles.

6 Tell him you were planning on paying for dinner.

> **WARNING:** YOU MUST TAKE ALL OF THE ABOVE ACTIONS WITHOUT GIGGLING, WHEEZING OR CONVULSING IN A FIT OF LAUGHTER. PRACTICE ON YOUR PET BEFORE ATTEMPTING THESE METHODS FOR THE FIRST TIME.

Celibacy Is Better Than Really Bad Sex

HERE'S AN OLD ADAGE OUT THERE — "EVEN BAD SEX IS BETTER THAN no sex." In my mind, this is like saying "spoiled, rotten hamburger is better than no meat at all." This is why it's okay to be a vegetarian — or celibate — sometime in your life.

However, if you haven't had a relationship — or sex — in a while, it's easy to feel like Tito at a Jackson family reunion. Like you're the only one who's not making it. So, for those times when the last wet spot you remember came from an excited puppy; when the last long, hard object you saw was dangling at a deli, just remember these *benefits* of being sexless in the '90s:

The joys of no-sex

- Turn extra condom cash into condo cash.
- Get full reprieve from discomforts of thong underwear.
- No worrying about sexually transmitted diseases, pregnancy or guys named Trevor.
- Guaranteed respect in the morning.
- Enough beauty sleep to turn you into Michelle Pfeiffer.
- An opportunity to watch Jay Leno all the way through.
- Clean sheets!
- More time to read inspirational books, like this one.
- The freedom to reacquaint yourself with Ben & Jerry.
- No need to buy *real* breakfast food as long as there's last night's pizza.
- No faking.

Keep the door open — but carefully examine whatever wanders in

Okay. Okay. So, maybe the Joys of No-Sex Guide doesn't make you feel any better about not being in a relationship. But remember, a relationship doesn't guarantee anything. A lot of married people are just as celibate as we are. The only difference is the joint income tax filing.

I'm not saying give up. I haven't given up. I've just discovered that a guy who irritates you at dinner will irritate you more in the morning. A fling for the sake of a fling won't make you feel any better the next day than eating two whole quarts of chocolate chip cookie dough ice cream. And waiting for something good is better than taking whatever's convenient — even if it means spending the night alone. Or, in my case, quite a few nights alone. But, I'm picky.

How to Meet a Really Wonderful Person

There were years when I got my dating allotment in before March, and still pegged it as a good year. There were times when I was still dateless in December. And it took me a long time to realize that there really wasn't anything "wrong" with me. It was those boneheads who passed me up for someone named Heidi. Or Heather. Or Mildred, for all I know.

But, I got to know a really wonderful person during those times. Myself. The same wonderful person, with or without a date. The same person who will one day find Mr. Right For Me. And put an end to this celibacy crap forever.

Just like you.

Single Is Better Than Anything I've Dated So Far

(and I've got pictures to prove it)

IN RETROSPECT, PARTICULARLY AFTER A COUPLE OF GLASSES OF Chardonnay, it's easy to start believing you let "Mr.-Right-For-Me" get away. Maybe mom, the nuns and the talk show guests were right. Maybe there are no "good ones" left.

That's when you need to take time out for past-date revue — an honest look at just what you've been bringing home all these years. Trust me, after a few minutes of these mental reruns, you'll feel much better about *still* being single.

How many of these flashbacks raise the hair on the back of *your* neck?

The Point 'n' Grin
"Why I'm Not Married, Mom"
Response List

MR. "LIFE IS A LEMON"

He had a bad childhood, a very bad adulthood, and a really bad day. He plans on aging poorly, if he's unlucky enough to live that long. He believes life sucks, the world is unfair, and the only joy in life comes from complaining. After one date with this man, you will surely contemplate escaping to the Ladies Room to hang yourself with your Sheer Energys.

MR. "IT'S MY PARENT'S FAULT"

He's perversely proud of his dysfunctional family — so proud that, even at his age, he still blames them every time you mention one of his flaws. If you've got a hard luck story, he'll always be ready to top it. And he thinks the guests on Oprah actually have nothing to complain about. After all, they haven't had *his* miserable life. Thankfully, neither will you.

Mr. "So Positive That He Causes Stomach Upset"

The bluebird of happiness obviously bit this man on the butt at a very early age. He hums incessantly, smiles at the evening news and will stop to smell every rose. He loves musicals, and secretly believes all families are like the Von Trapps. He's enough to make Maria consider going *back* to the convent — or you to consider entering one.

Mr. "Do I Have To Wear Shoes?"

He's casual and down to earth, that's true. But for this man, putting on a pair of pants is an attack on his personality. He prefers, instead, to hang out all day in his underwear, and believes the McDonalds' dress code is too strict. The only benefit to dating him? Your dry cleaning bills go way down. Then again, so does your libido.

MR. "JUST STARTED WORKING OUT"

He's in the throes of a mid-life crisis — of course, the divorce started that. Now he works out more than he showers, has sworn off red meat, red wine and any type of sex that doesn't get his heart rate into the perfect aerobic state. This includes foreplay. Before every date, he'll perform the fat pinch-test on your rear end, and keep a chart. He may lift weights, but he's the real dumbbell.

MR. "ME ME ME ME"

He begins every sentence with "I" and ends each one with "me." And if the conversation doesn't revolve around him — what he thinks or what he does — it's just not a conversation. He is his own best friend. He is his only friend. And he will most assuredly irritate you and all of your friends.

Mr. "Personality Like White Rice"

This is typically a nice guy — a very nice guy — who can't understand why nice guys like him can't find lasting relationships. He doesn't notice people slipping into comas as he drones on endlessly. He doesn't know why his last three girlfriends decided they were asexual after his first night with them. He is as much fun as matzo, with the energy level of a bookend. He is the equivalent of not dating at all.

Mr. "Over-Therapied"

This man likes — no, *loves* — therapy, has dated his therapists, can quote his therapists and exhibits his Prozac on his etagere. He also feels fully qualified to analyze you — from the color of your nail polish to your choice in breakfast cereal. He thinks you have a problem. You do. It's him.

Mr. "I Could Do Better"

This man has some strange need to give you great details about his dating history, will show you pictures of all his ex-girlfriends, and point out every woman at the mall who he thinks he could "make." He's pretty sure he could do better. You're one-hundred percent certain *you* can.

Mr. Milktoast

He loves your intelligence, your career and your independence, which is a pleasant switch. However, the thing he really loves is never having to make a decision, never doing anything on his own, and never having to take the blame when something goes wrong. He's the kind of guy who wouldn't make a peep if a smoke alarm went off. Escape before you have the urge to set him on fire.

Mr. "My Job's More Important Than Your Job"

He achieved success through hard work and perseverance.
You, on the other hand, must have gotten lucky. He belittles your
car, your college degree and your stock portfolio. He may be a great
breadwinner, but he's about as comforting as a yeast infection.

Mr. "My Children Don't Like You"

This man's life revolves around his children, to the
point where he'll believe the opinion of a kid
who's not quite potty-trained over that of
an Albert Schweitzer. He doesn't
discuss his love life with friends,
but with children who still stick
gummy bears up their nose.
Get away, before you're
dumped for a kindergarten
teacher.

Mr. "See You In Court"

He's been sued by his ex-wife, ex-employer, kids, parents and therapist. He's countersued, and the mailman, the dry cleaner and the neighborhood beagle are all on his list. After one date with F. Lee Jr. here, he's sure to lose his appeal.

Mr. "Angry Young Man Turned Forty"

The truth is, if this man had money, he'd be a yuppie. He's broke, so he's a rebel instead. He's constantly talking about "taking a stand," and "changing the world," but he's never registered to vote. His biggest cause is the helmet law. But when it comes to causes, realize that *he's* a lost one.

WHERE ARE THEY NOW?

There are others. Others who probably went on to live happily ever after — or ended up in prison, in the priesthood or pasted to barstools. There are some who had really great potential, and others I know were Mr. Wrongs, but still remember fondly. And then there are those I hope are going bald, wearing bifocals and saying, *"Yes, dear"* every five seconds to nagging wives. But one thing is for sure.

None of them was "Mr.-Right-For-Me."

Granted, being single isn't always rosy. But it sure beats waking up to any of those guys. Day after day. Year after year. Decade after decade. And whispering those three little words.

Oh-My-God.

To be followed by those four little words.

What Have I Done?

An enlightened friend once told me there'd be three men in my life: the man who loves me, the man I love, and the man I eventually marry. And although I scoffed at my friend's cynicism at the time, I can honestly say that, in my life, I've met the first two. It's the third one that keeps eluding me.

But, maybe — just maybe — I've had a better life because of it. And looking back, I can't think of a single moment that I'd trade.

Which brings me to my last rule: *It's okay to be single — even if you're over 30.* Who knows? It may give your life a humorous perspective.

Or, at least enough material to write a book.

Acknowledgements

I'd like to thank Rich Lippman for finally letting me experience his editing brilliance firsthand, even if I do hate it when he's funnier than me. And Joe Azar, an amazing illustrator and really nice guy, who always offers a word of encouragement. I'd also like to thank my parents, George and Claire Putnicki, for teaching me to deal with difficult situations through humor, and to always meet the deadline. And to Maggie Bundren, for always believing in me. I am also indebted to Patty Dzmura, Diane Van Dyk, Karen Callahan, Sarah Stevenson, Jan Stanley, Nancy Falter, Robin Harrop and Mary Lind Mahmud for listening to my tales of dating woe with the patience of Oprah, but without the words of advice. And to Gary Thurman, Richard Neal, Bill Hanley, Joe Stoniecki and Bryan Vanderslice for their ability to enlighten me with the male perspective. Not that it's helped. And to the Maldens, Rorabacks, Smiths, Carters and D'Entremonts for never saying, "if you don't hurry up, all the good men will be gone."

Finally, I'd like to thank Mr.-Right-For-Me, wherever he may be. And warn him that he'd better be worth the wait.

About the author

Patti Putnicki

Code name: SWF, VGL, AKA Box 413

Age: 35

Could pass for: 35

Home: Dallas, Texas (but she doesn't do trucks.)

Occupation: Author of *Man School* and *101 Things Not To Say During Sex*

Income-Producing Occupations: Marketing Director for a Fortune 1000 Company, freelance comedy writer for anyone who's willing to pay, and a variety of stand-up comedians who want you to think they wrote the material themselves.

Hobby: Dating

Frustration: Dating

Education: BFA, University of Texas/Dallas. Majored in theatre so parents would be *especially* proud.

Biggest Accomplishment: Turning 10 years worth of bad dating experience into a book.

☐ *YES!* Home-cooking sure tops celibacy!

NAME		DAYTIME PHONE NUMBER WITH AREA CODE
ADDRESS		APT. NO.
CITY	STATE	ZIP

Please send me the following books:

	How Many?	Price Each	Total Price
◆ *EATING IN — The Single Man's Cookbook*	____ x	$8.95 =	____
◆ *"It Was On Fire When I Last Checked On It."*	____ x	$8.95 =	____
◆ *CELIBACY Is Better Than Really Bad SEX*	____ x	$9.95 =	____
		Book Total	____
		Sales Tax (CT addresses only)	____
		Subtotal	____
		S&H ($3 per book)	____
		Order Total	____

Thank you!

Charge It! 1-800-243-0495

☐ MasterCard   ☐ VISA

Card Number _____

Expiration Date (mo/yr)_____

Signature _____

In Connecticut call toll-free: **1-800-962-0973**

Mail orders: Complete the charge card information above, or enclose check or money order payable to: *Globe Pequot Press*. Mail to: P.O. Box 833, Old Saybrook, CT 06475-0833.

Fax orders: Fax this form day or night with your credit card information: **203/395-0312**

In A Hurry?

Overnight or 2-day *RUSH* delivery is available for a small extra charge on phone orders only.
Call 1-800-243-0495

10-Day Money-Back Guarantee if not completely satisfied.

*If you're
looking for Mr. Right
back here,
you REALLY need
this book.*